"About forty-four years ago the Spirit gave me illumination of John 17 and Ephesians 4. I was undone. Yes, the prayer of Yeshua/Jesus will be fulfilled. We will be one and overcome the divisions, competition, separations, and lack of cooperative unity. We will be one **as He and the Father are one.** Then the world will believe that the Father sent the son. This book is a great confirmation. The prayer of Yeshua will be fulfilled."

DANIEL C. JUSTER, PH. D.
Founder Tikkun International.
A founding father in the Messianic Jewish movement.

"Jonathan's commitment to John 17 unity isn't just theoretical—I've personally witnessed him living out this message, demonstrating that it's achievable in our lifetime. This book is an invitation to boldly believe in the power of Jesus's prayer and to align our lives with His vision. As you read it, allow Jonathan's words to challenge your heart, removing any obstacles that prevent you from wholeheartedly embracing Jesus's call for unity."

JOEL MCGILL, teacher and YouTuber
www.youtube.com/@joelmcgill

Also by Jonathan Friz

10 Days: The Unlikely Story of a Global Movement Mourning for the Return of Jesus

JESUS
GETS WHAT HE PRAYS FOR

JONATHAN FRIZ

Copyright ©2025 by Jonathan Friz

All rights reserved.

No part of this book may be used or reproduced in any manner whatsoever without written permission, except in the case of brief quotations in critical articles and reviews. No part of this book may be used or reproduced in any manner for the purpose of training artificial intelligence technologies or systems.

Published by Presence Pioneers Media, Farmville, NC.

Cover design by Honour Frasier.

Printed in the United States of America.

Scripture passages taken from the ESV® Bible (The Holy Bible, English Standard Version®), copyright© 2001 by Crossway Bibles, a publishing ministry of Good News Publishers. Used by permission. All rights reserved.

Scripture passages marked NIV taken from the Holy Bible, New International Version®, NIV®. Copyright © 1973, 1978, 1984, 2011 by Biblica, Inc.™ Used by permission of Zondervan. All rights reserved worldwide. www.zondervan.com The "NIV" and "New International Version" are trademarks registered in the United States Patent and Trademark Office by Biblica, Inc.™

Scripture passages marked NKJV taken from the New King James Version®. Copyright © 1982 by Thomas Nelson. Used by permission. All rights reserved.

"The Prayer" Scripture passage taken from taken from the (NASB®) New American Standard Bible®, Copyright © 1960, 1971, 1977, 1995, 2020 by The Lockman Foundation. Used by permission. All rights reserved. lockman.org

ISBN (print): 978-1-951611-63-7

Dedication

To my dad.
3 John 4

Contents

Foreword by Gaylord Enns / vii
Introduction / 1

Part 1: Just as We are One
How is God one? And how can we possibly be one in that way?

    Chapter 1: Let Them Be One / 9
    Chapter 2: Before the Foundation of the World / 23
    Chapter 3: An Eternal Conversation / 33
    Chapter 4: Heavenly Union on Earth / 43
    Chapter 5: Collision at the Cross / 55
    Chapter 6: The Inner Life of God / 63
    Chapter 7: Into the Song / 75

Part 2: Same Game, Different Seats
Do other parts of Scripture foresee a glorious, united church? What historical precedents might prepare us for such a revolution? What might the fulfillment of John 17 look like?

    Chapter 1: Until Unity / 87
    Chapter 2: The Roadmap / 99
    Chapter 3: Experiential Knowledge of Love / 115
    Chapter 4: John 17, the Nations, and Israel / 127
    Chapter 5: Pioneers of Spirit and Sky / 141
    Chapter 6: Signs of Coming Glory / 155
    Chapter 7: The Fullness / 165

Part 3: In Pursuit: Seeking the Fullness of John 17
How should we pursue the fullness of John 17? What personal and corporate mindsets and practices are essential for divine unity?

> Chapter 1: Extraordinary Prayer / 185
> Chapter 2: Spiritual Unity and Structural Unity / 197
> Chapter 3: The Gift of Helps / 211
> Chapter 4: Divisions / 221
> Chapter 5: "Meditate on My Love for You" / 231
> Chapter 6: Choose the Lower Seat / 241
> Chapter 7: Lay Down Your Life / 253

Acknowledgments / 265

Foreword

If you have not already met Jonathan Friz, I am honored to introduce him to you. The son of a pastor, he was gripped in early adulthood by a passion to see churches come together as an expression of their unity in Christ. Unlike many with that idea, Jonathan began working to see that happen in his city, then across the USA, and now around the world.

My introduction to him came in 2010 when I was told that he had spoken about Jesus's new commandment—"Love one another as I have loved you"—at a Solemn Assembly in Plymouth, Massachusetts. My interest was immediately piqued because I had recently released *Love Revolution: Rediscovering the Lost Command of Jesus*. Within hours, I was calling him from California.

After our first conversation, I mailed two copies of *Love Revolution* to his home in Massachusetts. Jonathan and his wife Cassi read it at the same time and halfway through the book, she exclaimed, "Jonathan, you could have written this book!" Having gotten to know him better over the last fourteen years, I would agree!

I soon learned about the 10 DAYS movement that Jonathan had birthed in 2005. After we met, he visited my hometown of Chico, California and introduced 10 DAYS to us. It has deeply impacted our city and has been instrumental in bringing a growing unity among pastors and congregations.

His first book, *10 Days: The Unlikely Story of a Global Movement Mourning for the Return of Jesus,* was released in 2023. My wife Patti and I read it and our appreciation for Jonathan's passion and extraordinary commitment to the unity of believers before the return of Jesus was only deepened.

That brings us to his latest book, *Jesus Gets What He Prays For.* This book is a "must-read" for every pastor, Christian worker, and believer in Jesus Christ. It is a "now" word—a must for us at this time as we seek a fresh wind of the Holy Spirit that will awaken the global church!

I identify with Jonathan's passion for a global spiritual awakening. My personal life was forever changed when I was hit by an "early drop of the Jesus Movement rain" in 1965. That exploded in 1967 when I and two of the first hippies to receive Jesus in Northern California were welcomed into a small country church with the words, "We love you, we love you, we love you!" Within months, the place was packed to standing room only with new Jesus followers. We were united by God's love for us and our love for one another.

As you know, two thousand years of church history has not been a picture of unity. In this book, Jonathan's passion for unity has led him to explore the depths of what Jesus asked of the Father in the last hours before the cross. It was Jesus's prayer for His disciples then and for those of us living in this moment of history. This book is a seminal presentation that explores the necessity of this unity and what that could look like in your city and around the world.

Even as 10 DAYS has now become a global prayer movement, I believe this book will be used by the Holy Spirit to inspire the hearts and minds of believers worldwide to live out the reality of Jesus's command to "love one another as I have loved you." It will also motivate us to experientially become the answer to Jesus's prayer that we would be one just as He and the Father are one!

Foreword

Thank you for reading *Jesus Gets What He Prays For* and for being an answer to Jesus's prayer in John 17!

GAYLORD ENNS
Jesus Movement leader, pastor, and author of *Love Revolution: Rediscovering the Lost Command of Jesus*

Introduction

As long as I can remember, my imagination has been stirred by Jesus's prayer in John 17.

"Let them be one as we are one."

During childhood, I was shocked by the scandal of the church's division into 45,000 denominations. As a college student, I began to wrestle with the full weight of Jesus's prayer. How can human beings be one *just as* the Father is one with the Son? As a young man, the Lord dramatically called me to work for the unity of his church. Now, in middle age, I have been working for a fulfillment of Jesus's prayer for over twenty years.

As I began to write this book, making the case that "Jesus gets what He prays for," I was shocked at my own unbelief. I've been a champion of Jesus's prayer for my adult life. And yet, after all that time, my faith for its fulfillment was so small. Wrestling with the prayer of Jesus made it clear—I was a man of little faith. Writing has been an active process of repentance—a turning away from what my eyes see and growing confidence in what the Lord says.

As I've come into greater agreement with the heart of Jesus, Scriptural insight into the timing of the full answer to Jesus's prayer, and even the strategic importance of divisions in the church began to reveal themselves, I have found myself continually marveling at the Father's plan and Holy Spirit's abundant power to answer Jesus's dying request. God, as it turns out, is an excellent strategist. He is committed to answering the prayer of His Son and committed to doing it through His people.

While today we do not see the prayer answered in fullness, I believe we may be living in the generation that will see the perfect answer to this prayer. The result will be a spiritual revolution far more radical than the Protestant Reformation or Pentecostal Renewal. It will be an advancement for humanity much greater than the printing press, or the invention of powered flight. The full answer to Jesus's prayer in John 17 will change the world with end-of-the-age implications.

No wonder it has not happened yet, because when it does everything will change.

Until that time, we can experience increasingly powerful partial fulfillments every time we gather together with other believers, with the Spirit present among us.

As you read, my prayer is that God brings you through a similar process of repentance, a turning away from old and ragged thinking, and turning to the glorious truth: Jesus is going to get what He prayed for! And some of us reading these words may be alive long enough to welcome the new normal for His people on earth.

Jonathan Friz
November 2024

Introduction

The Prayer: John 17:1-26

Part 1: Jesus Prays for Himself (John 17:1-5)

    After Jesus said this, He looked toward heaven and prayed: "Father, the hour has come. Glorify your Son, that your Son may glorify you. For you granted Him authority over all people that He might give eternal life to all those you have given Him. Now this is eternal life: that they know you, the only true God, and Jesus Christ, whom you have sent. I have brought you glory on earth by finishing the work you gave me to do. And now, Father, glorify me in your presence with the glory I had with you before the world began."

Part 2: Jesus Prays for His Disciples in the Room (John 17:6-12)

    "I have manifested your name to the men whom you gave me out of the world; they were yours and you gave them to me, and they have kept your word. Now they have come to know that everything you have given me is from you; for the words which you gave me I have given to them; and they received *them* and truly understood that I came forth from you, and they believed that you sent me. I ask on their behalf; I do not ask on behalf of the world, but of those whom you have given me; for they are yours; and all things that are mine are yours, and yours are mine; and I have been glorified in them.

I am no longer in the world; and yet they themselves are in the world, and I come to you. Holy Father, keep them in your name, the name which you have given me, that they may be one even as we are. While I was with them, I was keeping them in your name which you have given me; and I guarded them and not one of them perished but the son of perdition, so that the Scripture would be fulfilled."

Part 3: Jesus Prays for His Disciples in the World (John 17:13-19)

"But now I come to you; and these things I speak in the world so that they may have my joy made full in themselves. I have given them your word; and the world has hated them, because they are not of the world, even as I am not of the world. I do not ask you to take them out of the world, but to keep them from the evil one. They are not of the world, even as I am not of the world. Sanctify them in the truth; your word is truth. As you sent me into the world, I also have sent them into the world. For their sakes I sanctify myself, that they themselves also may be sanctified in truth."

Part 4: Jesus Prays for Future Disciples (John 17:20-26)

"I do not ask on behalf of these alone, but for those also who believe in me through their word; that they may all be one; even as you, Father, are in me and I in you, that they also may be in us, so that the world may believe that you sent me. The glory which you have given me I have given to them, that they may

Introduction

be one, just as we are one; I in them and you in me, that they may be perfected in unity, so that the world may know that you sent me, and loved them, even as you have loved me. Father, I desire that they also, whom you have given me, be with me where I am, so that they may see my glory which you have given me, for you loved me before the foundation of the world. O righteous Father, although the world has not known you, yet I have known you; and these have known that you sent me; and I have made your name known to them, and will make it known, so that the love with which you loved me may be in them, and I in them."

Part 1: Just as We are One

How is God one?
And how can we possibly be one in that way?

1

Let Them Be One

Shrill and jarring, my alarm awakens me at 3:30 in the morning. Wiping sleep from my eyes, I crawl from my warm bed. I stumble to the bathroom, quickly brush my teeth, and grab my bag. My wife has risen with me to make coffee and kiss me goodbye as I leave for the airport.

I hate flying, but I'm a Christian. We're supposed to suffer with joy, or at least quiet dignity. I'm trying my best to have a better attitude.

After an hour's drive to the airport, I face the indignity of going through security. My carefully packed bag is unpacked, my shoes and belt removed. Who doesn't love an early morning pat-down to start the day?

Finally, we board the plane. My neighbor is listening to rap music at full volume on his phone, no headphones. It is not my favorite song. The baby two seats back is screaming at the top of her lungs.

"At least she's healthy," I think to myself. Needless to say, my long legs are not an asset onboard. In the middle seat, my knees are crushed into the seat in front of me—the seat whose thoughtful owner decides to recline.

Did I mention I hate flying?

Three hours later, as if by some miracle, we land safely more than 1,200 miles away.

The Impossible Possible

On December 17, 1903, on the remote sand dunes near Kitty Hawk, North Carolina, the Wright brothers made the first flight in an engine-powered, heavier-than-air vehicle—what we now call an airplane. The first fight covered a total of 120 feet and lasted twelve seconds.

Only five people were on hand to witness the revolution.[1]

For years after, many remained skeptical that the Wrights had ever flown. But, what was conceived in secret would soon transform warfare, exploration, and transportation, as well as the way we see ourselves in the world. It was less than seventy years from the Wright brothers' first flight to a photo of the earth from outer space. Tellingly, Neil Armstrong carried a piece of the Kitty Hawk Flyer with him as humanity set foot on the moon for the first time.

From Impossible to Normal

On January 1, 1901, the dawn of the twentieth century, no human being had ever flown. The testimony of thousands of years of recorded history was universally clear: powered flight is impossible. Pursuing it was vanity at best and probably madness.

The tenacious ingenuity of two bicycle-mechanic brothers and twelve seconds at Kitty Hawk changed everything. The gravity of thousands of years of human experience was not enough to hold them down.

For all of recorded human history, no one could fly. Today, human flight is so normal that it has become routinized, safe, and boring. What technological revolutions await us in the future, we may not know. However, as the story of the Wrights makes clear, realms of existence that were closed for the entire history of humanity can open quite suddenly.

---

1 David McCullough, *The Wright Brothers*

What is impossible today may become tomorrow's new normal.

John 17: The Impossible Prayer

John 17 is the longest prayer of Jesus recorded in the Bible. It's our most in-depth, most intimate glimpse into His communication with His Father. It was spoken on the night He was betrayed, the night before His death, in His greatest moment of crisis.

The prayer has a main theme: "[Let them] be one just as we are one."

After praying briefly for Himself (v. 1-5) Jesus turns His focus in prayer to His disciples, those who will carry His mission forward after He leaves. While He certainly has the apostles in the room in mind, He makes it clear in verse 20 that He is praying not only for those in the room, or for the first generation of believers, but "for those who will believe through their word."

He is praying for His future followers, for us. "[Let them] be one just as we are one."

The main theme of His prayer is repeated three times.

> v. 11 "I am no longer going to be in the world; and yet they themselves are in the world, and I am coming to you. Holy Father, keep [guard] them in your name, the name which you have given me, *so that they may be one just as we are.*"

> v. 20-21 "I am not asking on behalf of these alone, but also for those who believe in me through their word, *that they may all be one; just as you, Father, are in me and I in you, that they also may be in us,* so that the world may believe that you sent me."

> v. 22 "The glory which you have given me I also have given to them, *so that they may be one, just as we are one.*"

The thrice-repeated theme reaches a crescendo in verse 23, where Jesus prays for a perfected or mature oneness among His followers:

> "I in them and you in me, *that they may be perfected in unity,* so that the world may know that you sent me, and you loved them, just as you loved me."

In Jesus's longest prayer, He asks for something seemingly impossible:

> "[Let my disciples] be one just as we are one."

The Weight of the Prayer

The beginning of the gospel, John 1:1-3, describes how the Father and Son have existed in perfect unity from before the foundation of the world.

> "In the beginning was the Word, and the Word was with God, and the Word was God. He was in the beginning with God. All things were made through him, and without him was not any thing made that was made."

Before anything came into being, they were together in perfect communion. Everything in all creation springs from their union.

The Nicene Creed, the ancient statement of the Church that affirmed God's Trinitarian nature, declares that the Father and Son, while distinct persons, are "of one substance [or being]" with one another. They have different "personhood" but the same "being." The dynamic union between the Father and Son is the very substance that precedes, underlies, and sustains all that exists. Their union is so mysterious, intense, and intimate that we stretch language to its very limits to describe it: God is three persons with one being.

So that we don't miss the weight of what Jesus is asking for, let's translate Jesus's prayer into slightly different language.

Chapter 1: Let Them Be One

> "Father, I ask that you cause the human beings I've called out of the world to be united together *in the same way*, *to the same degree*, and *by the same means* that I am united to you. Let them be one with us and with one another just as we are one."

Let's spell it out even more:

> "Let them be one in the same way that we are one. Just as we are distinct persons with one fundamental being, let them be one."

> "Let them be one to the same degree we are one. Let the fire of their union burn with the same divine intensity that has united us from before the foundation of the world."

> "Let them be one by the same means we are one. Let's share the secret of our union with them, and catch them up in our fellowship."

Jesus is asking for created, fallen, and cursed human beings to be one as God is one with God. This prayer, quite simply, should not be possible.

The believer who is not offended by Jesus's prayer has not understood Jesus's words. Human beings cannot be one as God is one with God, can they? Everything in our experience screams that this cannot be true. The prayer not only contradicts our experience, it also seems to offend sound theology and the holiness of God. If anyone other than Jesus were saying "let people be one as God is one," we would consider it blasphemy. It sounds like a new-age heresy built on the oldest lie the devil ever told: that we can be like God.[2]

But this is Jesus. This prayer is Scripture. This is His heart cry to the Father before He goes to the cross.

---

2   See Genesis 3

Could it be that we are misinterpreting the prayer? Does it really mean what it seems to mean?

"Just As"

The whole power of the prayer depends on a comparison.

Jesus is not praying "Let them be one," full stop. If He were simply praying for His disciples to be united after He leaves, to have a good team dynamic and work together in His absence, we could conclude that He is a competent spiritual leader. He understands that "a house divided cannot stand." Coaches, generals, and businessmen all know the importance of unity.

He is not praying for His followers to have a good team dynamic and play well with others. His prayer is more specific. He wants them to be one in a certain way: "let them be one *just as* we are one."

Oddly enough, the meaning of the prayer hinges on the word "*as*."

The Greek word used here, *kath-os*, occurs 182 times in the New Testament and 31 times in John's gospel. Grammatically, it's a conjunction meaning "as," "just as," or "even as." The Greek word "*os*" is the equivalent of our English word "as," used primarily to make comparisons. *Kath-os* is an intensified version of *os*—it makes the comparison stronger, not weaker. In English we might say, "just as" or "exactly like" to intensify the comparison, making it clear that we don't just mean an approximation or a similarity—we're positing identity or near identity.

In modern English, we often prefer to use "like" instead of "as." "Like father, like son." If we wanted to intensify the comparison, we would say, "John is *just like* his father."

The Greek text is just as plain as the English. The comparison is clear: "let them be one *just like* we are one." He repeats the same prayer three times, emphasizing His point. Finally, in John 17:23, He sums it up: "that they may be perfected (completed) in one." Here, perfect oneness means the same oneness that Jesus and the Father have together.

The comparison makes the scandal clear: The plain meaning of the text is that Jesus is praying for His followers to be one *in the same way, to the same degree, and by the same means* Jesus is one with His Father. He wants His followers to have a union among themselves that is *just like* the divine union.

How can this be?

Three Scandals of Jesus's Prayer

Jesus's prayer is a scandal in three ways.

On the one hand, the prayer seems to trespass on God's holiness and separateness. In Isaiah 48:11, the LORD says, "My glory I will not give to another." We know that God alone is worthy of all honor, glory, and praise.

Now, in John 17:22, Jesus says, "I am giving my glory [to my disciples]."

The oneness of the Father and Son is central to the very nature of God Himself. It seems like a violation for God to share His holy, uncreated nature, His inner life with created beings, and especially with sinners.

God is God and we are not. We know this. How can we somehow share in the divine union?

On the other hand is the scandal of our experience. Neither 2,000 years of church history nor our personal experience with other believers display the divine oneness of Jesus's prayer. There are currently 45,000 Christian denominations. Even within those denominations, we know there are many disagreements and divisions. Of course, "one as we are one" is a much greater standard of unity than a mere lack of organizational division. Regrettably, our highest and best personal experiences as the church fall far short of the divine unity that Jesus requests.

Finally, there is the scandal of expectation. Are we to be one as Jesus is one with the Father? Is that the standard? If so, all of us are falling impossibly short. Have we even begun to follow Jesus? Once again, a brief tour of church history would suggest that we have always fallen short. How can God hold us to a standard that no generation has been able to meet?

Psalm 39 comes to mind, "LORD, I am a stranger with you, a sojourner like all my fathers. Turn your face from me, that I may smile again before I depart and am no more." This prayer is a burden too great for us, a standard too high for us. We are not better than our fathers.

Jesus's prayer puts us under tension. Everything in our lived experience, everything in our history, even much of our understanding of God is at odds with his prayer.

An Escape from the Tension?

Perhaps there is a way out. Perhaps we are not fully understanding the prayer in the right time and place.

Jesus's prayer means what it says. His disciples are going to be one "as the Father and Son are one." God is somehow extending His inner circle of fellowship to include redeemed humanity, but it's a serious mistake to think the prayer will be answered on earth, in this age.[3]

The prayer will be answered either in heaven after we die or after Jesus's second coming, in the age to come, either in the millennial Kingdom or in the new heavens and new earth, depending on your

---

3   "This age" is understood to be the period from Jesus's death, resurrection, and ascension until His second coming.

Chapter 1: Let Them Be One

theology. The prayer is still remarkable: how can human beings be one as God is one with God at any time, in any age? But at least the tension of expecting this divine union here and now, on this side of the Lord's return, is removed. The miracle can be hoped for in the future ages.

Jesus's prayer does not allow us this path of escape.

First, it is absurd to think of the Lord taking time from His own moment of crisis to pray for people in heaven. Never in Scripture do we see prayers offered for those in heaven. The saints above have already run their race and are cheering us on; they do not need our prayers. On the night of His betrayal, Jesus is not praying for those who have "fallen asleep" to be one.

Neither is Jesus's praying for a fulfillment after His second coming, in the age to come. Context makes it clear He is praying for His disciples now, in this age, before His second coming.

As He says, "I remain in the world no longer, but they are still in the world, and I am coming to you" (John 17:11a). He emphasizes the location of His disciples again in verse 15: "I don't pray that you take them out of the world, but that you keep them from the evil one."

The phrase, "the world" in John's gospel means much more than "the earth" or "the cosmos"—it's a term that specifically refers to the realm of creation that is not under God's rule. "The world" hates Jesus and hates His disciples—Jesus's disciples are not of "the world." Satan is the "world ruler" (John 14:30). While John does use "the world" more rarely to refer to the entire created order, as in the phrase "before the foundation of the world," it is clearly used here in the narrower sense.

Yet, Jesus prays for an answer to His prayer to manifest in full view of the unbelieving world.

> "Let them be brought to complete unity so that *the world* may know that you sent me and that you have loved them [my disciples] just as you loved me." John 17:23

The timing of the answer to the prayer is clear. It must be on earth and visible to unbelievers. His dying wish is that we would be one as He is one with the Father, shining like the sun into the dark night of this evil age.

We cannot escape the tension of Jesus's prayer. He is not praying for the cloud of witnesses in heaven or for a future time after He returns. He is praying for believers on earth, before He returns. He is praying for the church right now.

His Dying Request

In our household, we pay special attention to birthday requests. Requests that would be "no" on every other day are "yes" on their special day. Our children love this and try to stretch the day as far as they can. A birthday is good, but a birth-week, or birth-month is even better. Why not expand the season of favor as far as possible?

Special requests are also granted to the dying. The dying request of a beloved family member is almost always honored. Even the worst criminals, violent and vicious murderers, are granted special meals and other privileges before they are executed.

We see in John 17 that Jesus is preparing to offer His life as a redeeming sacrifice for every human being. To this point, He's perfectly executed His Father's plan. He's walked it out to the letter. Now, He's about to land the *coup de grace* against the forces of darkness at the cost of His own life.

Do you think, on this night of all nights, His Father might be paying attention, granting special favor to His beloved Son? There is no doubt that the Father in heaven is taking careful note of everything Jesus requests on this night, recording it in heaven, and moving heaven and earth to answer His Son's dying request.

Of course, the intensification of the night is hardly needed. We know that God always answered Jesus's prayers when He was on earth. For one thing, Jesus only did what He saw the Father doing, and only said what He heard the Father saying. His prayer life was a perfect representation of the Father's will.

There is only one moment recorded in Scripture where God did not do exactly what His only-begotten Son asked, and it's the exception that proves the rule. It was actually a prayer He prayed later that night.

When Jesus prayed, "Father, let this cup pass from me, *but not my will, but your will be done*," He tipped us off to the fact that He was not praying God's will. You'll notice, it's only here at His most vulnerable, most human that He ever prays "not my will, but your will be done." Jesus didn't walk around praying, "Father, heal this leper, but not my will but your will be done." He simply declared God's will: "Be healed."

From the simple fact that Jesus prays for it, we know the Father's answer must be, will be "Yes." If that is true of any of Jesus's prayers, how much more so of His dying request?

The Unavoidable Truth

Here's the unavoidable conclusion of Jesus's prayer: Jesus gets what He prays for.

The impossible prayer of Jesus is going to be answered in fullness before He returns. Jesus's prayer is prophetic: it will have a fulfillment. Jesus's disciples will be one, as He is one with the Father. If it has not happened yet in fullness, we must look to the future. His words will not, cannot fall to the ground.

Jesus's prayer may not fit with our theology. But His prayer is good theology—we should adjust to how He sees things. If we have seen Jesus, we have seen the Father. If you have heard Jesus pray, you know what the Father is going to do.

Proof of Union

Jesus is going to get what He prayed for. But how will we know if His prayer has been answered, partially or in fullness?

Thankfully, He gives us an external sign, a proof of union that will enable us to know when His prayer has been fully answered. The external proof is in John 17:23:

> "Let them be brought to complete [perfect, mature] unity so that *the world* may know that you sent me and that you have loved them [my disciples[4]] just as you loved me."

When Jesus's prayer is fully answered, the testimony of the oneness of His followers will be so powerful and undeniable it causes the unbelieving world to recognized Jesus as the one who was sent by the Father.

As a secondary effect, it will cause unbelievers to recognize Jesus's disciples as those who have been loved by the Father just as the Father loved Jesus.

This "proof of perfect union" is parallel to the "proof of discipleship" Jesus gave earlier: "by this all men will know you are disciples, by your love for one another" (John 13:35). John 13:34-35—the New Commandment to "Love one another just as I have loved you"—is the beginning; John 17:23—becoming "perfectly one"—is the end goal.

In giving His proof of union, Jesus wants the world to recognize who He is. This makes perfect sense; after all, "every knee will bow and

---

4   A common mistake here is to misread the pronoun "them" as referring to "the world." In John 17, the third person pronouns (them, these, they) always refer to Jesus's disciples, and never to the world. God does love the world (John 3:16) but that's not what is being said here. Jesus is saying the same thing He will say in John 17:26, that the love He experienced from the Father would be in believers so that the entire world would see that His followers are the beloved of God.

every tongue confess that Jesus Christ is Lord."[5] However, it is striking that He also wants the world to recognize who we are.

Why are we included along with the Lord? Why does He want the world to recognize who we are, and how much we are loved by the Father?

I often tell people they do not fully know me until they meet my wife. I'm not fully myself when she is not around. Apart from her, I am only partially known. Similarly, Jesus is so identified with us as His bride, that He is jealous for the entire world to know us and to see how much the Father loves us. He's not fully himself without His Bride, the one for whom He laid down His life. Jesus wants the world to know Him and to see His beloved.

The Days Before Flight

We will know when Jesus's prayer in John 17 is fully answered.

There is going to be a revelation of heavenly union on earth among God's people, something that will be visible and undeniable to the unbelieving world, and will cause them to recognize that Jesus has been sent by God.

Without a doubt, there have been and will be many partial fulfillments of John 17. However, the ultimate fulfillment will be a historical event. The whole world will see who Jesus is—they won't be able to deny it. And everyone will confess His people are the beloved of God.

We will know when we arrive. Our enemies will let us know. They will see Jesus and His Bride, the church, as we truly are and be unable to deny what they see.

In terms of Jesus's prayer, it's January 1, 1901. We are living in the days before flight.

---

5   Philippians 2:10-11

Today, we do not see the church visibly one as the Father and Son are one. Those who hate God often mock us; they are not in awe of our unity.

Don't believe what your eyes see. Don't believe what your ears hear. Don't allow the weight of 2,000 years of history to tie your faith to the ground. The Father has never forgotten Jesus's prayer. He holds it continually before His eyes. He has never stopped moving to answer it, not for one second of history. Jesus gets what He prays for. We are moving inexorably toward this future unity. This is our new normal.

The Father is going to answer Jesus's prayer.

2

Before the Foundation of the World

A flock of a thousand starlings takes flight at the same moment. Soon, the entire group is performing a complex display of synchronized flying, without any planning or apparent communication.[1] Shapes undulate in and out, like a swirling work of modern art. The entire mass seems controlled by a central mind. Individual birds make sudden, tight turns, and yet none of them collides, lands, or leaves the group. The flock moves in complex but effortless unity. Then, all at once, the display is over as each individual bird lands within seconds of one another.

Our minds can grasp wild geese flying in "V" formation. However, we have no idea how starlings coordinate their infinitely more complex movements. The flock seems to be led by the same mind, like a single organism composed of countless individuals, anticipating one another's movements and flowing together without a leader. Are the birds one or many? Does a flock somehow have a common mind?[2]

How are a flock of birds one?

One of the strongest proposals comes from the field of chaos theory. Perhaps each individual bird follows a few very simple rules: Don't hit

---

    1   https://www.americanscientist.org/article/flights-of-fancy for one example of many describing this fascinating and still elusive natural phenomenon.
    2   *Thought-transference (or what!) in birds,* Edmund Selous, 1931.

other birds, stay close to the nearest birds, and fly in the same direction and speed as neighboring birds. And yet, while the computer models using these inputs are similar, they're not an exact match.

The answer remains elusive to modern science. We still don't understand how a flock of birds is one.

How is God one?

"Let them be one **as we are one**."

To understand Jesus's prayer, we must understand how the Father and the Son are one. Their union is the deepest mystery in all of existence. If it's hard to understand how a flock of birds are one, how can we hope to understand the unity of God?

And yet, if we don't understand something of their union, we have no idea what Jesus is praying for. To understand how God is one, we are going to have to go back to the very beginning.

Actually, we need to go back even further.

To understand how God is one, we need to go back before the beginning.

The first verse in the Bible starts at the beginning.

> "In the beginning, God created the heavens and the earth." Genesis 1:1

Genesis 1 goes on to share the origin of everything in all of creation. It's the story of how it all started.

Somehow, the gospel of John begins even earlier. It starts before the foundation of the world.

> "In the beginning was the Word. And the Word was with God, and the Word was God. He was in the beginning with God. All things were made through Him, and without Him nothing was made that was made." John 1:1-3

Prequel

The gospel of John and many other Scriptures speak to a remarkable reality—there was a "beginning" before the beginning. The story that begins in Genesis with creation has its origins in an even older story, the story of the inner life of God.

This is the beginning of all beginnings, the story of the love that unites the Creator to Himself. Everything in creation flows out of who God is, out of His nature. John 1:1-3 reveals that everything we see flows out of the loving union of the Father and the Son.

Astonishingly, this is the same union that Jesus prays we will have with one another.

If we want to understand what Jesus means when He says, "Let them be one as we are one," we need to go back with Him before the foundation of the world. We need to understand how the Father and the Son are one.

God's Inner Life: Colossians 1:15-20

Paul's letter to the Colossians contains one of the most beautiful expositions of the relationship between Father and Son:

> "*He [the Son] is the image of the invisible God, the firstborn over all creation. For in him all things were created*: things in heaven and on earth, visible and invisible, whether thrones or powers or rulers or authorities; all things have been created through him and for him. He is before all things, and in him all things hold together. And he is the head of the body, the church; he is the beginning and the firstborn from among the dead, so that in everything he might have the supremacy. *For God was pleased to have all his fullness dwell in him,* and through him to reconcile to himself all

things, whether things on earth or things in heaven, by making peace through his blood, shed on the cross." Colossians 1:15-20

In John 14:9, Jesus says "He who has seen me has seen the Father." In Colossians 1, we hear this same reality declared, "[The Son] is the image of the invisible God." The Son is the perfect likeness of Father God. If you have seen Jesus, you have seen the Father.

As in John 1:1-3, we learn that "all thing have been created through [the Son] and for Him." However, not only are all things created through Him, but they also are continually held together by His agency, "in him all things hold together" (Col. 1:17). So, the Son and the Father have a dynamic partnership both in creating and maintaining the universe.

Colossians 1:19 summarizes the eternal relationship between Father and Son this way:

> "For it pleased God [the Father] that in him [the Son]
> all the fullness should dwell…"

The Son is the exact image of the Father, the one who possesses all the fullness of God.

If you want to know what the fullness of God is, look to the Son—all the fullness is living in Him. The Father has entrusted the full measure of His power, authority, love, nature, and glory in His Son, holding nothing back in the least.

God's Inner Life: The Nicene Creed

In the first five hundred years of Church history, controversy swirled as the people of God wrestled with how to understand the mysterious unity and multiplicity of God. This period of upheaval was tied to a historical event: God had become a man. All prior categories were exploded by this one fact.

Chapter 2: Before the Foundation of the World

Led by the Holy Spirit, these early believers gifted us new language and statements of faith to help us summarize the testimony of the Scriptures. We owe these believers, most of them forgotten on earth, a debt of gratitude. We are standing on their testimony.

Fundamentally, these early believers were wrestling with this problem: There is only one God. And yet, we know that the Father, Son, and Holy Spirit are all distinct. How are we to understand the oneness of God and the three-ness of God? In gatherings of senior Christian leaders (Church Councils) in Nicea (325) and Constantinople (381) they agreed and passed down the Nicene Creed, a confession laser focused on how to understand the Trinitarian paradox.

Today, we use the word "Trinity" to speak about the "Tri-Unity" of God. God the Father, God the Son, and God the Spirit are all distinct *Persons*. However, they all share a common "essence," "substance," or "being." Fundamentally, they are one. As distinct Persons, they all have different roles and personalities. We can speak of them separately. However, beneath it all is a fundamental Oneness. They are one God.

The eternal relationship between the Father and the Son is difficult to understand—should we be surprised since it precedes the creation of all that exists? And yet, passages like Colossians 1:15-20, John 1:1-18, and John 17 give us detailed information about God's eternal nature. The Nicene Creed synthesizes the testimony of Scripture into a single statement.

We will look at several sections in detail to help us understand the union between God the Father and God the Son.

The Union of Father and Son

"We believe in one God, the *Father*, the Almighty, maker of heaven and earth, of all that is seen and unseen."[3]

---

3   There are many English translations of the Nicene Creed. I'd encourage the

God the Father is the creator of all things visible and invisible. This is the first theme of the Creed, simple and strong. However, the nature of the Triune God becomes more intricate, complex, and beautiful as the Son is described.

> "We believe in one Lord, Jesus Christ, the only *Son* of God, *eternally begotten* of the *Father*, God from God, Light from Light, true God from true God, *begotten, not made*, consubstantial with the Father. Through him all things were made…"

John 1:18 calls Jesus "the only begotten[4] Son, who is in the bosom of the Father…" John 3:16 says that God gave "His only begotten Son" to the world so that anyone who believes in Him would have eternal life.

The Nicene Creed picks up on this theme, emphasizing that the Son is "eternally begotten" of the Father.

This language is strange to us, even if we have spoken it hundreds of times. What does it mean? Let's unpack the language of the Creed phrase by phrase.

"Father and Son"

The biblical language suggests sameness as well as difference in personhood and authority. In human relationships, a father and son are "the same kind of thing." And yet, clearly, the father is the source of the son and is greater in authority than the son. Jesus repeatedly

---

reader to examine several to get more perspective on these deep concepts. I'm using the 1975 ecumenical version (ICET).

4   Most modern translations render "only begotten" as "one and only". This is to avoid the "temporal" implications of begetting, which the Creed does through the phrase "eternally begotten." Some argue that "One and only" is a better reading of the original Greek, but this ignores how anyone who spoke Greek at the time would have read the word. "One and only" also separates us from our historic creeds.

communicates both His equality to the Father in one respect, "I and the Father are one" (John 10:30) and the Father's superiority in another respect, "The Father is greater than I" (John 14:28).

"Eternally Begotten"

This strange phrase means that while the Son comes from the Father (the Father is the source), the Son of God has always existed with the Father—there was never a time when He did not exist. In fact, it is a serious error to say that there was a time when the Son of God did not exist. And yet, He also comes forth from the Father. While this is hard to understand, few have explained it better than C.S. Lewis:

> "Imagine two books lying on a table one on top of the other. Obviously, the bottom book [A] is keeping the other one [B] up…Now let us imagine that both books have been in that position for ever and ever. In that case B's position would always have been resulting from A's position. But at the same time A's position would not have existed before B's position….The Son exists *because* the Father exists: but there was never a time *before* the Father produced the Son."[5]

The Son exists because of the Father, but there was never a time where the Son did not exist. Their relationship is eternal, without beginning or end.

"Begotten not made"

The Son of God is not a created being. He is Begotten.

While begotten is not a word we use in modern English, we need it to understand John's gospel and the Creed. "To beget" speaks to conceiving children. Human beings can make or create many things:

---

5 Lewis, C.S., *Mere Christianity* (New York: Harper Collins, 1952).

furniture, poetry, ships, houses, but they only *beget* other human beings. Birds make nests, and bees build hives, but they only beget birds and bees.

Likewise, God the Father can only beget something of like nature to Himself. Human beings are created by God. We are made, not begotten. However, the Son of God is fully divine and was not created like everything else in the universe. The Son of God is "God from God, light from light, true God from true God." He is begotten, not made.

"Consubstantial with the Father"

The mystery of God's nature is deep, and as our forebearers wrestled with it, it led to the development of new language. "Consubstantial" is a word custom-designed to describe the Trinitarian life. It means the Father and the Son are fundamentally and at the very bottom, one. Their being interpenetrates, they are inseparable from one another, they are one at the deepest level. While they are distinct Persons, they share a single, fundamental being or substance. Other translations render the same phrase "of one being" or "of one essence" with the Father. These phrases are all trying to describe the same reality. Just as Jesus said, "I and the Father are one."

"Through Him all things were made"

This final section signifies that while the Father is the Creator of all things, He creates all things through the Son. His activity in creation is never separate from the Son's activity.

This biblical theme begins in Genesis 1, where the Spirit of God and the Word of God are present in the Creation. The Son is the Word spoken by God that has created all things. "All things were made through Him." The Father's creative power is always exercised through the Son.

Before the Foundation of the World

It is surprising we can say anything about what happened before the foundation of the world. And yet, Scripture has a surprising amount to say about the Father and Son's relationship before creation.

The Father and Son have existed eternally, along with the Holy Spirit, in perfect unity. While this union is essential, core to their very being, we can also see that it is not a monolithic, undifferentiated unity. Rather, their union is multifaceted, complex, and personal. The Godhead is a fundamental and eternal union of three persons, Father, Son, and Spirit. The Father is the source of the Son—and yet, the Son is the perfect likeness of the Father.

Unbelievably, Jesus is praying for us to be brought into and included in this uncreated, eternal union.

> "Just as I am in you [Father], and you are in me, let them be in us [Father and Son]" (John 17:21)

We have only begun to understand how the Father and Son are one. Next, let's dive into the text of John 17:1-5 to see if we can learn more about their union. We'll do so by listening to a conversation they've been having since before the foundation of the world.

3

An Eternal Conversation

My wife, Cassi, is one of five sisters. Before we were married, I visited her family and was invited to play Taboo, a word-guessing game, with the girls. The goal is to get your team to say a specific word without saying several related words which are "taboo." I was more than happy to play. I'm highly competitive and usually good at word games. However, rather than showing off for my bride-to-be, I was about to be shown up.

Because Cassi and her sisters had lived together for years, they had thousands of shared experiences. Sometimes they'd just say a single word with no apparent relation to the target word, and the others would immediately guess the correct answer. Because they had grown up in the same household, they had an immense reservoir of shared experience that was completely inaccessible to me. Rather than impressing my fiancé as I hoped, my team lost badly.

Spending long periods of time with someone creates a large volume of shared experiences. Some people know each other so well, they seem to share the same mind. They can easily anticipate what the other is thinking or desires in almost any situation.

But what if instead of decades, we imagined people who had known one another for thousands of years, or even for an infinitely long time? What would they talk about with one another? What would it be like to listen in on their conversation?

Jesus Prays for Himself

In John 17:1-5, Jesus prays to the Father for Himself.

The Father and the Son have been in dialogue from before the foundation of the world. Incredibly, we get to listen in on an eternal conversation.

What does God talk about with God? What does the Word say to the one who spoke Him? What untold mysteries are exchanged between Father and Son?

According to John 17:1-5, they talk a lot about something called "glory."

> "Jesus spoke these things; and lifting up His eyes to heaven, He said, 'Father, the hour has come; *glorify* Your Son, that the Son may *glorify* You, even as You gave Him authority over all flesh, that to all whom You have given Him, He may give eternal life. This is eternal life, that they may know You, the only true God, and Jesus Christ whom You have sent. I *glorified* You on the earth, having accomplished the work which You have given Me to do. Now, Father, *glorify* Me together with Yourself, with the *glory* which I had with You before the world existed.'"

Glory

Jesus asks His Father to "…glorify the Son so that the Son may glorify You." He points to His obedience to fulfill His mission on earth, and repeats and intensifies the prayer in v. 5: "…and now, You, Father, glorify me together with Yourself with the glory that I had with You before the world existed."

In this beautiful prayer, Jesus also reveals a stunning definition of eternal life: "…and this is eternal life, that they might know you, the only true God, and Jesus Christ whom You have sent." To have eternal life[1] is to know the Father and the Son.

Jesus's deepest desire for Himself is to receive glory from the Father. This is the same glory He had with the Father before the world was made. It is incredible how Jesus is quick to bring up shared experiences with the Father from before creation!

As Jesus shared earlier in the gospel of John, the right way to live is not to receive the glory of men, but rather the glory of God (John 5:41-44). Here, He expresses His desire to receive glory from His Father, while unveiling to the Father how all His activity on earth has all been to glorify Him.

We can summarize Jesus's prayer this way: "I have glorified you. Now glorify me, so that I can glorify you."

Apparently, when the Father and Son speak, a transfer of glory, back and forth between them, is at the forefront of their mind. But what is "glory"? And why is Jesus so concerned with both giving and receiving glory?

Moses, Man of Glory

If we were looking for a person from the Bible other than Jesus who walked closely with God, Moses would be on our short list. Just as the Father trusted Jesus to institute the New Covenant, He trusted Moses with the Law. Both Jesus and Moses walked with God in a way that amazed their contemporaries.

Interestingly, we find Moses praying a very similar prayer in Exodus 33:18. In this passage, Moses reveals the deepest desire of his heart to God:

---

1 The phrase "eternal life," common in John's gospel, speaks of both abundance and duration. So, this not only means "forever life" but also "abundant, overflowing life." While this life is often (rightly) presented as referring to the eternal ages to come and as being realized after we die, it is clear from here and many passages in John's gospel that "abundant, forever life" begins now, whenever the believer receives it.

"Please, show me Your glory."

It is remarkable that both Moses and Jesus know to ask for the same thing.

In Hebrew, the word translated "glory" is the word *kabod*, which carries the sense of "weight" and "heaviness." The glory of a thing conveys its weight. And God Himself is supremely heavy. Unlike Jesus, Moses has never seen the glory of the Father. But he is close enough to God to know seeing His glory is what he wants above all else.

Moses asks to see God's glory. And God responds this way:

> "I will make all my goodness pass before you and will proclaim *my name, Yahweh*...but, you cannot see my face, for man shall not see me and live." Exodus 33:19-20

Moses asks to see God's glory, and God responds by speaking about His goodness, His name, and His face. However, the glory or "weight" of God is too great for Moses to bear. "You cannot see My face, for no man can see Me and live." It is clear by the way He responds that God's goodness, name, and face are all closely related and synonymous with the glory of God. They are all overlapping concepts.

Moses will not be able to see God face-to-face. An unmediated encounter with the uncreated one would be fatal for Moses. However, he will be allowed to see God's "back." In a striking display of intimacy, God covers Moses with His hand in the cleft of a rock until it is safe for Moses to gaze upon God and not die.

When God appears to Moses in glory, He declares His Name to Moses:

> "The LORD [Yahweh, God's covenantal name] descended in the cloud and stood with him there, and proclaimed the name of Yahweh... 'Yahweh, Yahweh God,

merciful and gracious, slow to anger, and abounding in steadfast love and faithfulness. Keeping steadfast love for thousands, forgiving iniquity and transgression and sin, but who will by no means clear the guilty, visiting the iniquity of the fathers on the children and the children's children to the third and fourth generation.'"
Exodus 34:5-7

When God reveals His glory, He declares His name, revealing His nature and character to Moses.

Weighty Glory, Shining Glory

When Moses descends from the mountain, his face is *shining* from the encounter with God's glory, and it terrifies the Israelites.

> "Now it was so, when Moses came down from Mount Sinai (and the two tablets of the Testimony were in Moses' hand when he came down from the mountain), that Moses did not know that the skin of his face was shining while he talked with Him. So when Aaron and all the children of Israel saw Moses, behold, the skin of his face shone, and they were afraid to come near him."
> Exodus 34:29-30

In this passage, we see a different Hebrew word for glory, *qaran* translated here as "shining." *Qaran* is closely related to the Hebrew word for "horn," as in the horns of an animal. Because of this, it is common in medieval art to see Moses coming down the mountain with literal horns coming from his head. While this may seem funny to us, this image of Moses with horns on his head can help us understand this second Hebraic idea of glory.

Kabod-glory speaks of the weight or heaviness of something. More weight, more glory.

Qaran-glory is what proceeds out and becomes visible from something, the way horns come out of an animal. More radiance, more brightness, more glory.

This same idea, "to proceed out and become visible" is also conveyed by the Hebrew word *halal*, most commonly translated "praise" but also translated "glory." This is the root of the word *hallelujah*, and it literally means "to shine forth." The Greek word *doxa* which is the primary word for "glory" in the New Testament has a similar root meaning. In this sense, glory is what proceeds out from something or someone in a positive sense, displaying and revealing their true inner nature.

For instance, light and heat proceed out from the sun, but they are not the sun. We can say that light is the "glory of the sun." Trees and grass are the "glory of the earth" because they proceed out from the earth and display its goodness. In this sense, a desert land lacks glory. When talking about people, the word "honor" or "reputation" is a synonym for "glory." Speech proceeds from people just as sunlight proceeds from the sun. "Your reputation precedes you." Words about us go before our actual presence. If you've ever wondered what Paul is talking about in 1 Corinthians 11 by saying "woman is the glory of man," he's saying that woman proceeded out of man in creation according to Genesis 2. Similarly, hair is glory because it proceeds out of the head.

In conclusion, the glory of something is its inner nature made visible and perceivable to those outside. We can understand glory as "weight," "gravity," or "heaviness" (*kabod*), and also as what "shines forth," "radiates, or "proceeds" (*qaran, doxa*) from something.

Moses was desperate to behold the glory of God. It was his deepest desire. When God revealed His glory to Moses, He declared His name. His name spoke to His character and nature, including His goodness, patience, lovingkindness, faithfulness, and justice.

Knowledge of the name of God is knowledge of who God is. And this knowledge is eternal, abundant life. This is exactly what Jesus prays in John 17:3, "This is eternal life, that they know you, the only true God…" Of course, the kind of knowledge Jesus is speaking of here is not book learning or head knowledge. It's not information you can research on the internet. It's the experiential knowledge of God, an encounter with the glory of God, and revelation of the name of God. It's the kind of knowledge that might kill you or make your face shine for days. It's the kind of knowledge that comes from beholding the glory of God.

Moses's cry to God, "show me your glory," is the prayer of a man who knew God better than any living human being at that point in history. However, this longing for revelation of the glory of God is not unique to Moses. In fact, many of those who were closest to God in the Old Testament had a similar hunger.

Consider the prayer of David, the man after God's own heart:

> "One thing I have asked of the LORD, that I will seek: that I may dwell in the house of the LORD all the days of my life, to gaze upon the beauty of the LORD and to inquire in His temple." Psalm 27:4

Moses, David, Jesus. Somehow, those who are close to God all have His glory as the deepest desire of their hearts.

The Glory Exchange

> "Father, the hour has come; *glorify* Your Son, that the Son may *glorify* You." John 17:1b

While great saints like Moses and David knew beholding the glory of God was the "one thing" to be desired above all others, there is a significant difference between them and Jesus. Jesus has an eternal history with the Father. He has beheld the Father face-to-face eternally. What would have killed Moses is normal for Jesus. He needs no protection from the full revelation of God's glory. The Father's glory is His native country. He and the Father have the deepest history together. He is speaking about what He knows.

Interestingly, He does not just desire to see the Father's glory like Moses and David.

> "*I have brought you glory* on earth by finishing the work you gave me to do. And now, Father, *glorify me in your presence* with the glory I had with you *before the world began.*" John 17:4-5

He longs for the Father to give glory to Him.

"Father, glorify the Son…"

However, the Son is not simply a recipient of glory from the Father. He seems to want to receive glory only so He can return it to the Father.

> "Glorify the Son so that the Son may glorify you."

The deepest desire of Jesus's heart is to experience an exchange of glory, back and forth, between Himself and the Father. He wants to give glory to the Father and receive glory from the Father. He wants to behold the Father's glory, and He wants to return that glory to the Father.

> "Glorify me, so that I may glorify you."

And again,

> "Glorify Me with the glory I had with you before the world began."

The Father gives His glory to the Son, and the Son gives the glory He received back to the Father, who then returns it to the Son, and

Chapter 3: An Eternal Conversation

so on. We will call this circular, back-and-forth movement of glory between the Father and Son *the glory exchange*.

Whenever Jesus speaks about the glory exchange, He is reminding the Father of experiences they shared before the foundation of the world. The glory exchange has no beginning in time and will have no end. However, Jesus is also clear to point out that the glory exchange has entered a new phase when He became a man.

"I have brought you glory on earth…"

The glory exchange that has been eternal in the heavens is now taking place between heaven and earth. The exchange is eternal, but through the incarnation of Jesus Christ, the location of giving and receiving has changed. Earth is now on the receiving end of the glory of God.

While the glory of God is fascinating, the most fascinating thing in all of existence, the question remains: what does the glory of God have to do with the union of Father and Son? What does the glory exchange have to do with the oneness of God? And, how on earth are we ever supposed to be "one as the Father and Son are one"?

4

Heavenly Union on Earth

The sun is an immense nuclear fusion furnace turning hydrogen atoms into helium and releasing massive amounts of energy, giving life to our entire world.[1] The fusion of immense amounts of hydrogen into helium in the sun is the reason you're reasonably warm and able to read this page.

Under normal circumstances on earth, hydrogen will not fuse into helium. Hydrogen atoms may form chemical bonds with many other types of atoms, for instance, oxygen, to create water. However, two hydrogen atoms hanging out next to each other on planet earth will never become helium. They'll maintain their distinction and probably form chemical bonds with other elements.

The sun is 333,000 times heavier than the earth. Gravity on the surface of the sun is twenty-eight times the gravity of the earth, and it's much higher at the sun's core, where fusion is most active. Because of the sun's immense mass, hydrogen is put under incredible pressure, especially at the center of the sun.

The key elements for a fusion reaction are intense pressure and intense heat and light. Immense amounts of pressure (weight) combined

---

1 The actual process of hydrogen to helium fusion is a bit more involved, however this simplified description is accurate. Information for this description was taken from https://en.wikipedia.org/wiki/Nuclear_fusion.

with incredible light and heat (a core temperature of 15 million degrees Celsius) create the perfect environment for fusion to take place. To translate these scientific ideas into biblical ones, it takes an unearthly amount of *kabod* (weighty-glory) and *qaran* (shining-glory) to create fusion in the sun.

What we think of as "normal" is simply what we are used to on earth. Fusion is normal in the heavens. It happens continually and our earthly life depends on it. In contrast, on earth it seems virtually impossible.

And yet, building off the heavenly pattern in stars, fusion on earth has been achieved numerous times. Terrifying hydrogen bombs briefly create the conditions of the sun right here on the earth. It is hoped that one day, fusion power will be mastered by scientists in a less destructive form, leading to abundant, clean, inexpensive energy for the entire world. At the time of this writing, fusion power remains "ten years away"[2] but there is reason to hope we will live to see the power of the heavens on earth.

One thing is certain, if fusion power ever becomes normal on earth as it is normal in the heavens, everything will change.

Heavenly Union on Earth

After Jesus finishes praying for himself in John 17:1-5, He begins to pray for His disciples (John 17:6-26).

The main theme of the prayer is "Let them be one, just as we are one." But, the question remains: how can human beings be "one as the Father and Son are one"?

The answer is surprisingly straightforward: to achieve the unity of heaven on earth, we need what makes the Father and Son one in heaven, on earth. We need the fusion power of heaven to operate on

---

[2] A common joke among scientists is that fusion power is always "ten years away."

earth if people are to be one in the same way and to the same degree as the Father and Son are one.

In John 17:6-26, Jesus makes four special petitions for His disciples, requests based on His knowledge of God's inner life, that reveal His plan to make us perfectly one.

Petition 1: Guarded in the Father's Name (John 17:6-13)

> John 17:11 "I am no longer in the world, but they are in the world and I am coming to you. Holy Father, *guard*[3] *[keep, protect] them in your name, the name you have given to me, so that they may be one just as we are one.*"

As we have already seen in Exodus 33, the name of God is closely related to the glory of God. When Moses asks to see God's glory, the LORD declares His name to Moses. As we think about the exchange of glory between Father and Son, we might also think of it as a name exchange—the Father declares His name to the Son, and the Son in return declares it back to the Father.

Jesus is bold to say the Father's name has been given to Him (John 17:5,11-12). This name is part of the fullness of God He received before the foundation of the world. Now, as the rightful and full possessor of the Father's name, He asks for His disciples to be protected, guarded, or kept "in the name." Just as the Son possesses the Father's name as a free gift, now He gives it freely to His people, and requests the Father to guard His people inside the name.

Where Are We?

Jesus's strange manner of speech, "guard them in your name," makes it seem like the Father's name is a place. We think of being "in" a house, a car, a city, or a nation. As a father, I often think of guarding my kids as

---

3 The Greek word *tereo* is translated as "guard," "keep," or "protect."

they swim or play on a playground. We might think of guarding people in prison, making sure they do not escape.

Strangely to us, Jesus speaks of the Father's name as a place and asks the Father to make sure we never leave. John 1:18 says:

> "No one has seen God at any time. The only begotten Son, who is in the bosom of the Father, He has declared Him."

For Jesus, the name of God is a place—before He took on flesh, it was the only home He had ever known. His home is the bosom of the Father, the place where He sees God face-to-face. Jesus has captured us like spoils of war and brought us into His home as His prized possessions. We belong to Him now, and Jesus is asking His Father to guard us within His name, to not allow us to leave His name or allow anyone to take us from His name. Why does Jesus want us to be with Him, resting in the name of the Father? So that we can be one with one another as He is one with the Father.

The bosom of the Father is the only place where this union is possible. It's why we always see the disciple Jesus loved leaning on Jesus's chest. He's giving us an example: stay within the divine embrace. Remain in the name. The name is the only place where union is possible.

Just as natural fusion in the sun is contrary to our earthly experience, so life within the Father's name is unfamiliar to our earthly minds. What we think of as normal, that two people are separate and distinct beings, does not apply inside the Father's name. Within the Father's name, we retain our distinction as persons and yet share a common being and essence. We are in the Son, the Son is in the Father, we are in one another. Inside the Father's name, we are one.

Even though we are remaining in the world in our bodies, Jesus is asking the Father to bring us into His bosom by the Spirit, so that we

Petition 2: Set Apart in Truth (John 17:14-19)

> "My prayer is not that you take them out of the world but that you protect them from the evil one. They are not of the world, even as I am not of it. *Sanctify[4] [set them apart, make them holy] in truth*. Your word is truth. As you sent me into the world, I have sent them into the world. For them I sanctify myself, that they too may be truly sanctified." John 17:15-19

As Jesus continues to pray for His disciples, He asks the Father to leave them in the world, the realm of existence under the control of Satan, but to "keep [guard, or protect] them from the evil one." Jesus has shared the Father's word with them, and they have received it. They are not of the world, just as Jesus is not of the world. He is sending them out into the world just as the Father sent Him (v. 15, 18). Over and over again, the disciples are portrayed as replicas of Jesus, receiving all He has received, doing what He did, and being sent as He was sent.

In verse 17, Jesus prays, "Sanctify them [set them apart, make them holy] in truth. Your word is truth."

The Greek word rendered "truth" (*alethia*) can also be translated as "reality" in English.

God's word is the underlying substance of reality. Everything that we perceive as "real" is composed of words spoken by God (Genesis 1:3, John 1:1, Hebrews 11:3). Jesus wants the disciples to be set apart and made holy in the Father's reality. This is especially important because the disciples are remaining in "the world," a realm of lies and deception.

---

4   The Greek word *hagiazo* can mean "to make holy," "to set apart," "to consecrate," or "to sanctify." It is the normal word used for "holiness" in Greek.

The ruler of the world is a liar, so being set apart in the truth is especially necessary in such a hostile environment.

Just as Jesus's disciples are kept and guarded within the Father's name, they are also made holy, cordoned off in truth, which is the Word of God. As with the Father's name, we get the sense that truth is a place, a walled garden where protection from the evil one is guaranteed by the Father's watchful eye. As Jesus prepares to leave them and return to the Father, He is making sure His followers are protected and cared for, guarded by the name of the Father, and set apart in "the truth." While this second petition is not directly linked to Jesus's prayer for unity, there can be no doubt that apart from the truth, such divine union is impossible. Truth, holiness (or sanctity), and unity are all closely-related concepts. How could there be divine unity among those who are living in the unreality of Satan's lies?

Finally, Jesus makes the radical claim that He "sanctifies Himself" for the sake of His disciples. He has set Himself apart for a special purpose—He has made Himself holy to keep them in the truth. Here, Jesus is not speaking about moral purity. He is referring to His sacrificial death. By laying down His life, He will set Himself apart for their sakes. His voluntary sacrifice of everything is offered upward, in obedient love to the Father and outward, for the benefit of His beloved disciples.

Petition 3: Glory: An Uncreated Gift (John 17:20-23)

As Jesus's prayer reaches a climax in John 17:20-26, we find the specific petition for His followers to be "one as we are one" repeated twice in just a few lines.

> "I do not pray for these alone, but also for those who will believe in me through their word; *that they may all be one,* as you, Father, are in me, and I in you; that

they may be one in us; that the world may believe that you sent me. *And the glory which you gave me I have given to them, that they may be one just as w are one*: John 17:20-22

In verse 22, Jesus declares that He is giving His glory, the glory that the Father gave Him, to His disciples. This glory is essential to divine unity.

Before the foundation of the world, the Father shared His glory, His fullness with the Son—the Father has given everything He has to the Son, with the sole exception of His own headship that comes from being the Source. Jesus strongly desires both to receive glory from the Father and to give glory to the Father (John 17:1-5).

And yet, how can it be that God's glory would be given to human beings? In Isaiah 42:8, we hear this: "I am the LORD, that is My name; and My glory I will not give to another…."

We know that God's glory belongs to Him alone. Even with a Trinitarian understanding of God's inner life and how glory is exchanged between Father and Son, we still understand that this is the glory of God. It is His nature. His substance. How can it be shared with human beings?

And yet, here Jesus says:

> "I am giving them my glory which you gave me, so that they may be one as we are one."

Verse 24 makes it clear, if there was any question, that Jesus is referring to the glory He received from the Father "before the foundation of the world."

This glory is uncreated, it is *kabod*, the weighty glory of God's presence. It is *qaran*, the shining glory of God's radiance. Just as the sun's weight, light, and heat causes the fusion of hydrogen into helium, in the same way, this uncreated glory unites Father and Son in perfect union. It is the glory that makes God three persons with one being. Now, Jesus is bestowing this same glory on human beings, so that they can be one in the same way. How can this be?

Where Can We Experience this Glory?

As we read on in verse 23, we see that Jesus living in us, and the Father living in Jesus, will ultimately result in our perfect union in Him, causing the world to recognize Jesus's true nature.

> "I in them and You in Me; that they may be made perfect in unity, that the world may know that You have sent me, and have loved them as You have loved Me."
> John 17:23

In characteristic language that reflects the heavenly reality, Jesus makes it clear there is only one "place" where His disciples can experience this glorious, uncreated union.

Jesus is in the Father, and the Father is in Him. To be "one as the Father and Son are One" with each other, His disciples will have to enter into the inner life of the Trinity. The degree of oneness that Jesus is speaking about is only present in God, and only possible in God. Somehow, through the gift of the glory He received from the Father, Jesus is inviting His disciples to enter the inner life of God, the bosom of the Father.

Humanly speaking, to even imagine such a thing seems blasphemous; we are creatures, and He is our creator. And yet, we are not imagining it—the Son of God is praying for it. The Father is moving even now to answer the cry of His Son. God has initiated this divine union that seems too good to be true. Let us not draw back in unbelief.

Lest our faith fail, and we refuse to believe our own eyes and ears because of the magnitude of what He is asking, the prayer somehow gets even better.

Petition 4: Love: Standing in Jesus's Place (John 17:24-26)

As He concludes the prayer, He sums it up this way:

> "I have declared your name to them, and will *continue to* declare it, so that the love with which you loved me may be in them, and I in them." John 17:26

This final prayer is almost unbelievable. Jesus wants us to experience the Father's love just as He Himself experiences His love. He wants us to stand in the place where the Son stands within the Trinity and experience the full force of the love of God, just as if we were Jesus. He wants the love of the Father that has lived in Him from before the foundation of the world to take up residence inside of us.

Let's imagine we are Moses, standing on the mountain before the glory of God, except here Jesus is saying, "Not just your back, let them see what I see, what I have always seen, let them know your love as I have always known it."

Jesus is praying, "I want them to stand where I stand. I want them to experience what I experience. I want them to receive your love, just as I receive your love and know your love just as I know your love. This is the eternal, abundant life I want them to receive."

Summing Up John 17:6-26

As He prays for us, Jesus first brings us into the name that has always been His home, into the bosom of the Father, asking the Father to keep guard on us, to put us under lock and key so we are not able to leave His name.

He sets us apart us in heavenly truth as a bulwark against the world that surrounds us, the same reality He has always known as the Word of God.

He welcomes us into the inner life of God, invites us into the place where He is in the Father, the Father is in Him. Now we are in the Father and Son, and they are in us.

He bestows on us His glory, the uncreated glory He received from the Father before the foundation of the world.

Finally, He asks the Father to reveal His love to us in the same way and to the same degree He has always known the Father's love.

Proportionate Means

Jesus has asked for something impossible: for human beings to be one as the Father and Son are one. However, the impossible prayer is backed up with proportionate means.

Jesus is not envisioning mere human beings walking in supernatural unity on their own. He is offering heavenly help, supernatural help. In fact, this help is beyond supernatural. He is offering divine and uncreated means to His disciples. He is promising to give us the very bond of union between Father and Son in heaven here on earth, making us one in the same way, to the same degree, by the same means.

And He is willing to go to the cross to make the Uniter available to us.

Where is the Holy Spirit in Jesus's Prayer?

It may seem odd to the reader of Jesus's prayer that the Holy Spirit is never mentioned by name. After all, isn't God a Trinity, three in one? Why is the third person of the Trinity never mentioned as Jesus prays for unity? Why does Jesus seem to describe divine union as existing between Father and Son, and not as between Father, Son, and Spirit?

Chapter 4: Heavenly Union on Earth

And yet, Holy Spirit has been present all along.

Jesus is bold to pray "Let them be one as we are one" because He knows when He ascends, He will pour out the very Spirit of God to inhabit His followers. The same Love that binds Father and Son, the same Glory whose radiance fuses Father and Son in perfect, heavenly union, is the same Spirit who will fill His disciples in just a few days' time.

The Spirit is the Name, the Glory, the Truth, the Love of God. We can think of these as different names for the Spirit, different functions of His ministry, or as different manifestations of the Spirit. He is the one who makes the Father and Son one. He is the only one who can make us one as they are one.

Looking from the outside, we might imagine the Trinity as a mysterious unity of three persons with equal functions. We might prefer to say, "one as the Father, the Son, and Spirit are one."

However, Jesus describes the union of God differently. The trinitarian life is the union of Father and Son *by means of* the Holy Spirit. The Spirit is a person, but His function is not like the Father or the Son. He is the one "who proceeds from the Father,"[5] the shining forth of His inner nature. He is the one who is constantly in motion back and forth between Father and Son, constantly burning, constantly moving, carrying the name of God back and forth. He is the Spirit of Truth. He is the living Flame of Love.

Fusion in the sun is a creation picture of the divine union. On earth, we know that each person has their own "being"—two people cannot become one being, just as we know that hydrogen atoms sitting next to one another will never become helium. However, in the heavens, our earthly logic falls apart.

---

5   See John 15:26 and the Nicene Creed (381 A.D. version)

As in the sun, it is glory that creates fusion in the divine nature. It is the *kabod* (heavy glory) and *qaran* (shining glory) of the Spirit that make Father and Son one. The Glory Spirit is the perfect bond of divine union. The Father is in the Son, and the Son is in the Father by means of the Spirit. This is how the three persons of the Trinity can be one being.

Jesus prays an impossible prayer: "Let them be one as we are one." Then, He makes an equally impossible promise: "I am giving them my Glory."

He offers proportionate means to make the impossible possible. He will pour out the uncreated bond of heavenly union on earth. He will send Holy Spirit to inhabit His people. He will welcome us into God's inner life.

And yet, this impossible prayer and impossible promise come at a terrible cost.

To make us one, the Son of God must die.

5

Collision at the Cross

Located near Geneva, Switzerland, the Large Hadron Collider is the world's largest and most powerful particle collider.[1]

Consisting of a circular tunnel seventeen miles in circumference, the Large Hadon Collider uses 10,000 magnets to accelerate beams of subatomic particles to .999,999,990 the speed of light. Because it is impossible to accelerate any object with mass faster than the speed of light, this speed is at the absolute edge of what is possible. To achieve these dizzying speeds and get peak performance from the magnets, the entire area is supercooled to -271.3 degrees Celsius, just two degrees warmer than absolute zero. When it is in operation, the LHC on its own requires about one-third of the electricity needed for the entire city of Geneva.

As these beams of subatomic particles are accelerated to immense speeds in opposite directions, they collide at extremely high velocities. Beams of particles are moving so quickly they circle the seventeen-mile circumference at a speed of 11,245 rotations per second.

Batteries of detection equipment measure the results, taking subatomic snapshots of spectacular, head-on collisions.

---

1 Websites consulted for this illustration include the Wikipedia page for the Large Hadron Collider as well as articles on space.com and home.cern on the LHC.

The Large Hadron Collider was designed to function at the very limits of the physical universe. Its extreme design is also incredibly expensive, costing $4.5 billion to build and $5.5 billion annually to operate. Why would anyone build such a thing?

The physicists who constructed the LHC were looking for answers about the underlying nature of physical reality. When sub-atomic particles are subjected to extreme conditions and collide, they break open, revealing even smaller particles with strange names like quarks, muons, bosons, and mesons.

The LHC is best known for experiments confirming the existence of the "Higgs Boson," the so-called "god particle" predicted by physicists, but never observed. It took extremes of size, speed, energy, and cold along with careful observation and perseverance (a forty-year search before it was observed), to reveal the existence of this elusive particle. But eventually, when matter collided under these extreme conditions, the secret inner workings of nature were revealed.

As human beings, our minds are habituated by how things work "normally," within our limited realm of common experience. However, what is normal for us conceals a deeper, stranger underlying reality. Reality at the sub-atomic level is nothing like our day-to-day reality. In fact, it's so different that it's difficult to even talk about it.

The Large Hadron Collider offers a simple lesson for us: sometimes it takes extreme circumstances to reveal something's hidden nature.

The Incarnation and the Cross

What if, instead of studying what is hidden deep inside created matter, we wanted to reveal what is deep inside the Creator? What if we were not looking for the "god particle" but for God Himself? Could it be that if we viewed God in the most extreme situation that the glory of God would be revealed and His hidden nature made visible?

Stunningly, John 1:14 makes the claim that the Son of God became flesh, a created human being.

How is it possible for the one through whom "all things were created" to become a created being? How can God become a man? As unbelievable as the incarnation is, it was only the first step in a costly, extreme experiment that makes the Large Hadron Collider look like a child's microscope kit.

God become a man. That seems extreme enough. But what would happen if the God-man died? Nuclear war or even the death of our earth's sun by supernova would be a minor occurrence by comparison. If God were to die, it would be a collision extreme enough to shake the very foundations of the universe. Would His death destroy everything? How could a new creation ever emerge from such chaos?

Death and Glory

In John 12:23-25, Jesus says:

> "The hour has come that the Son of Man should be glorified...Most assuredly, I say to you, unless a grain of wheat falls into the ground and dies, it remains alone; but if it dies, it produces much fruit. He who loves His life will lose it, and he who hates his life in this world will keep it for eternal life."

Yet again, Jesus is speaking about glory. And yet, it is clear here that Jesus is speaking about His upcoming death on the cross.

How can the hour of death also be the hour of glory? Dying on a cross is not glorious in any normal sense of the word. Quite the opposite, it is the ultimate moment of shame, torment, and humiliation. And yet, mysteriously, Jesus refers to death on a cross as His moment of glorification.

JESUS GETS WHAT HE PRAYS FOR

In John 13:31-33, on the night before his crucifixion, Jesus speaks about His glorification again.

> "Jesus said, 'Now the Son of Man is glorified, and God is glorified in Him. If God is glorified in Him, God will also glorify [the Son] in Himself, and glorify [the Son] immediately…Little children, I shall be with you a little while longer. You will seek me, and as I said to the Jews, 'Where I am going, you cannot come,' so now I say to you."

Once again, Jesus is using cryptic language and talking about glory.

His disciples did not understand His riddle until after He rose again. Because we know what comes next in the story, we are in a better position to understand. We know He is about to go to the cross. After that, He will rise from the dead by the power of the Spirit. Forty days later, He will ascend to Heaven. Jesus clearly refers to His ascension when He tells His disciples, "Where I am going, you cannot come."

When Jesus says, "Now the Son of Man is glorified," He must be speaking about either His death, His resurrection, or His ascension to the Father's right hand. His resurrection and ascension seem more like "glory" in the normal sense of the word. Which of these three moments is His moment of glory? Or, is it possible that the riddle of John 13:31-33 refers to all three moments?

Here it is again with extra words added to unlock Jesus's mysterious speech:

> "Now [at this very hour, the hour of His death], the Son of Man is glorified [by His death] and God [the Father] is glorified in Him [though His death]. If God [the Father] is glorified in Him [through death], God will also glorify Him in Himself [through resurrection and ascension] and glorify Him immediately [He will ascend to the Father soon after He dies]."

John 13:31-33 refers to all three moments: His death, His resurrection, and His ascension. All are moments of glory. The interplay between these three monumental events has brought us once more to the "glory exchange" between Father and Son.

"The Son of Man is glorified [by death]"

Jesus is glorified in His death.

Glory is the "shining out" and the "revealing" of something's true nature. It is on the cross, the most extreme and costly collision in history, that God's true nature is cracked open, revealed for all to see.

Jesus did not receive honor at that very moment, it was a moment of shame. But through deepest shame the Son of Man reveals the inner life of God, the greatest glory in the universe.

As Jesus said of His death in John 12:32, "If I am lifted up from the earth, I will draw all peoples to myself." The revelation of God's inner life on the cross, His faithful love, His humility, His kindness, and His justice[2] is so powerful that thousands of years later, it continues to draw people to Jesus. Jesus continues to receive honor and glory today, from heaven and earth, because of His death on the cross.

"The Father is glorified in [His death]"

Jesus's death not only reveals God to human beings. It reveals the full extent of the Son's obedient love to the Father.

From eternity past, the Son has been the recipient of the Father's fullness. He has possessed all the glory of God. On the cross, the beloved Son of God fully returns everything He has received back to the Father. He returns the glory to His Father. This is why the Father

---

2   Thinking back to Exodos 34:5-7 and the declaration of God's name to Moses, we must see the cross as the most complete, glorious, and compelling declaration of His name in history.

is glorified. He is receiving every bit of the glory He gave the Son back from the Son.

When Jesus says, "Father, into your hands I commit My Spirit," He is returning to Father God everything He received before the foundation of the world in obedient love. The Father receives all His glory.

"God [the Father] will also glorify [the Son] in Himself, and glorify Him immediately"

The glorious death of the Son deeply impacts the heart of Father God. The uncreated Son has become a grain of wheat, laying down His life in obedient love for the Father. In response to His Son returning every bit of the glory He received, the Father can hold back no longer. He glorifies the Son again. Stunningly, the result of this fresh explosion of glory from Father to Son begins an entirely new creation.[3]

Just as it was before the foundation of the world, the Father sends His Spirit and speaks forth the Son, bringing Him into Resurrection life. Once again, He declares "Let there be light!" and a new creation dawns. In just a few days, the Son ascends to heaven and is glorified again in the Father's direct presence, taking His seat at the Father's right hand.

The Father has been glorified in the Son's death. Now, He glorifies the Son in Himself through resurrection and ascension, and does it immediately.

The Cross and the Inner Life of God

The Cross is the most extreme collision in the history of heaven and earth.

---

[3] This is a rich New Testament theme, but Galatians 6:15, 2 Cor. 5:17 and other passages speak to this reality. The resurrection of Jesus on the first day of the week is a clear sign that a new Creation has begun.

Chapter 5: Collision at the Cross

The Father created all things through the Son. How can the creator be killed by His creation? And yet, the Son of God is crucified, murdered, and hung shamefully on a tree.

As His body is torn, the veil in the earthly temple is ripped open, unveiling the holy of holies,[4] the most inaccessible place on earth, where God's presence rested. This presence was so powerful and fearful that it could only be approached once a year by one man, the high-priest, and only through a blood sacrifice. The cross of Jesus rips the veil in two, symbolizing the ending of the Old Covenant, and dawning of a New Covenant, a covenant of continual access to God's glorious and immediate presence.

As Jesus's body is torn open, a window is also opened for the first time into the inner life of God.

The Father and the Son have an eternal relationship, an intimate, dynamic love for one another without beginning or end. Through the collision of the cross, Jesus is reveals the glory of their inner life, the beauty and wonder of their generous and humble love for one another.

As His body is torn, the inner life of God, the glorious reality that has existed continually from eternity past shines forth from His wounds. In the agony of His death, the beautiful music of God's inner life, known only to the Father, Son, and Spirit, begins to sound forth for all creation to hear.

However, the collision of the cross does not simply allow us to gaze into God's inner life, like stunned stargazers witnessing a supernova, or scientists studying particle collisions at the Large Hadron Collider.

---

4 In the Old Testament system, the holy of holies was the place where the Ark of the Covenant, the seat of God's presence, was kept. This area of the temple was inaccessible to everyone except one special man, the high priest, and he could only enter once a year to sprinkle blood. The holy of holies was separated from the rest of the temple by an extremely thick veil. When Jesus died, the veil in the temple was ripped from top to bottom, symbolizing that the inaccessible presence of God would now be available to all.

The cross reveals something far more spectacular: We are invited into the holy of holies, the place of God's manifest presence. Now, human beings are welcomed into the song, called to fully participate in God's inner life. We are now to be one, just as Father and Son are one.

6

The Inner Life of God

Concertgoers crowded into the chapel at Concordia Lutheran Seminary in St. Louis.

A brown, variegated stone exterior with a square steeple opened into an expansive worship space, with vaulted ceilings, stone floors, and high stained glass. I found my seat near the front of the church, on the far right.

About fifty singers and musicians arranged themselves in rows before the altar. The dull roar of hundreds of independent conversations suddenly hushed. The conductor, rising to his place, stilled the crowd with a flick of his wrist. With another flick, a wave of sound crashed over us.

"Kyrie Eleison"

The first movement of Bach's Mass in B-Minor is a mournful lament, "Lord, have mercy."

The lines of music wove together in harmony and deepest tension. The beauty of what sounded like a funeral march was immersive, all-encompassing. The music knew me better than I knew myself. I felt like I could go without happiness forever to keep experiencing the beautiful sadness of the first movement. And that was just the beginning.

As the first part of the Mass neared an end, a bass soloist, accompanied by french horn, bellowed out:

"For you alone are the Holy One. You alone are the Lord. You, Jesus Christ, alone are the Most High."

Suddenly, breaking in out of nowhere, the choir and orchestra erupted at full volume:

"*Cum Sancto Spiritu in gloria Dei Patris. Amen.*"

"With the Holy Spirit to the glory of God the Father. Amen."

As the Holy Spirit was invoked, He fell on the room.

For a skeptical teenager with very little personal experience of God, that moment went beyond the beauty of music. God was there. He was immanent. I felt I was experiencing the music of Father, Son, and Spirit, the inner life of the Trinity right before my eyes. In that moment, I knew God was real. As the piece ended, I thought my heart would explode from my chest. All of us rushed to our feet, erupting in praise and applause. The crowd became a united congregation, praising God with one voice.

There is a unique connection between music and the presence of God.[1] In the book of Revelation, we read that God's throne in heaven is constantly surrounded by musicians playing instruments and singing songs. Many of the songs of heaven are recorded word for word. King David, who was a prophet, tried to model his kingdom on God's heavenly Kingdom. He did this by pitching a tent, placing the Ark of the Covenant, the seat of God's presence, in the center, and arranging 24/7 worship and praise music around the Ark.

Think about it: God could have anything He wants surrounding His throne in heaven. Why does He have music?

---

[1] Matthew Lilley's excellent book, *David's Tabernacle,* delves much deeper into this mysterious connection between God's heavenly government and music.

Perhaps because music uniquely communicates the unity and diversity of the Trinity. Perhaps God loves music because the inner life of God is a song.

The Movements of God's Inner Life: A Thought Experiment

> "In the beginning was the Word. And the Word was with God, and the Word was God. He was in the beginning with God. All things came into being through him…" John 1:1-3

We might paraphrase John 1:1-3 this way:

> "Before the beginning there was a song. The Father sang it to the Son, and the Son sang back to the Father. The song was the inner life of God."

There was never a time before the song started. And yet, like any song it has a beginning, middle, and end. The chorus follows the verse. One movement leads to the next movement. As created beings we are entering the eternal song already in progress. And yet, incredibly, we can still discern the distinct movements of the music.

Let's do a thought experiment.

Let's use John 17 and the other Scriptures to map out the major movements of God's inner life. Let's see if we can describe the song the Father and Son have been singing since before the foundation of the world. Of course, there are many things about God's inner life we don't know and could never understand. There are many details of their life that have not been revealed. Our understanding is partial.

In a similar way, a road-map can never show every detail of the roads, trees, or buildings of an area. Maps are always partial. However, like a map, our description can be true, accurate, and helpful if we stick close to the testimony of Scripture.

Movement 1: The Father's First Act

We know the Triune God is eternal with no beginning or end. We also know the Father and the Son have a relationship before creation that is characterized by an exchange of glory between one another. This glory exchange is at the forefront of Jesus's mind as He prays for Himself in John 17:1-5. We know the Father is the initiator within the Trinity. He is the source. The very names "Father" and "Son" clearly communicate this reality.

Even though there was never a "first time," let's imagine the Father being aware of Himself as if it were the first time He was conscious.[2] He would immediately perceive His glory, greatness, His total power and blessedness.

No sooner is the Father aware of Himself, His name, His glory, His goodness and all that He possesses, than instantly He has a shocking desire. His deepest desire is to give everything that He has to another.

We could understand the Father wanting to share some of the glory of who He is, but this is not His desire. He wants to give everything—the fullness. In a stunning act, He gives all His fullness, all of His "Godness" to another, the only Begotten one, the Son of God.

The Father's first movement is to beget a Son in His own image, to give His fullness to another. He sends forth His Spirit, and the fullness of His love goes forth to fill His Son with the same glory that fills Him.[3]

---

    2   To be incredibly clear, because Father and Son are both eternal, uncreated, there was never a "first time." This thought experiment is put in human terms so that we can attempt to wrap our minds around it. The Son is "eternally begotten of the Father" as the Nicene Creed rightly states.

    3   The begetting of the Son is parallel to the creation of Adam. Genesis 2:7 "Then the LORD God formed the man [Adam] of the dust from the ground, and breathed into his nostrils the breath of life, and man [Adam] became a living soul." In both cases, it is the going forth of God's breath or Spirit that conveys life.

This "first movement" is what Paul is describing when He says, "He is the image of the invisible God, the firstborn of all creation…for it was the Father's good pleasure for all the fullness to dwell in Him."[4]

This is what Jesus was remembering when He prayed, "Now, Father, glorify Me…with the glory I had with you before the world was."

While there is no "before" this moment (and I want to be very clear about that), this is the first movement in the divine song. The Father gives all His glory, all His love, all His life, all His light to another one, the Only Begotten Son. This is what it means for the Son to be "in the bosom of the Father." It's to be the recipient of the fullness of the Father's name, reality, love, and glory for all eternity.

Looking at it from the outside, we might consider the Father's first act to be reckless and irresponsible.

Would it not make more sense to keep His divine nature to Himself? Or, if it was to be given away, to give only a portion of Himself? What compels Him to give the fullness of His "Godness" to the Son? And how will the Son respond?

Movement 2: The Son Receives the Father's Gift

As the fullness of God's nature is revealed to Him, we can imagine the Son "waking up" as from a deep sleep, becoming aware of Himself immediately as the beneficiary of all the love, glory, and power of the Father.[5] He would first encounter the mind-bending splendor, glory, and beauty of the Father. The Son would be completely overwhelmed by this vision of glory, overpowered by unapproachable light.

He would simultaneously know that He Himself now has "equality

---

4   Colossians 1:15, 19
5   The parallelism with Adam's creation in Genesis 2 continues. As best I can tell, this is intended and Adam's creation was modeled on the begetting of the Son of God.

with God"[6] and that He has done nothing to deserve it—it has come as a free gift. All the attributes of the Father are now also His. The Son is the happy recipient of all the glory, beauty, and honor of the Father. He rightly recognizes Himself to be the Father's equal in every respect, except for priority. He has the fullness of God!

How will the Son respond to the Father's gift? How could the Father take the risk of giving everything to another?

Movement 3: Returning Glory

The Son is completely overwhelmed by the Father's beauty, glory and generosity. He does not consider this indescribable gift, equality with God,[7] as something to be grasped onto or held with a tight fist. He does not hoard the fullness of God to Himself, even though the Father has given it to Him. Instead, in gratitude and praise to His Father, overwhelmed by His glory, beauty, and generosity, the only thing the Son can think of doing is to give everything He has received back to the Father.

Like His Father, He holds nothing back.

He empties Himself and commits His Spirit to the Father.[8] He returns the fullness of God that was given to Him back to God the Father.

The Glory of the Cross and God's Inner Life

We often think about the cross from the perspective of our need and God's love for us. And that is one part of the story. However, another part of the story is this: The Father and the Son existed forever in eternal blessedness in the unity of the Holy Spirit. They had no need to create. No need to make man in their image.

---

6 Philippians 2:6
7 Continuing to reference Philippians 2
8 Luke 23:46

The Son had no need to become a man and die a horrific death. And yet, Father and Son chose this path from before the foundation of the world.[9]

Why?

The collision of the cross reveals in history what has been true for all eternity. The Son gives the Father everything, holding nothing back.

The revelation of the Father's glory stirs the Son to go deeper still in humility before the Father, to go to the very depths, lower than low before the Father, to return even more glory to the Father. This has always been His desire as a true Son. But the Son's humility is a response to the Father's own stunning generosity. The Father, in His foolish wisdom, risked everything[10] by bestowing His fullness on another. The humility of the Father is found in His generous gift of EVERYTHING to the Son.

What if the Son had not responded as He did? What if He had grasped the fullness, kept it for Himself, instead of returning it? Many human and spiritual beings have had powerful encounters with God's glory and later tried to keep it for themselves. The stakes are high, and the risk is real.

The Song Continues: From Glory to Glory

Let's return to the song of God's inner life, as it continues to swell.

The Father's first and best desire is to beget a Son, to give all of His nature and likeness to another, to make one equal to Himself in all but ultimate authority. He takes what we might consider the ultimate risk in bestowing EVERYTHING He possesses upon another, the Son.

---

9   1 Peter 1:20 and other passages.

10   Some people are uncomfortable talking about God "taking a risk" because they feel it contradicts His omniscience. God, of course, does know the end from the beginning. However, the shape of the movement is the shape of an extreme risk. As we shall see, this form of risk has another name for us and in God's inner life.

The Son responds to the Father's extravagant generosity with deepest gratitude: He returns EVERYTHING the Father gave Him back to the Father.

And now, somehow the Father finds that against all logic, His own blessedness and joy has INCREASED.

The Son, the one to whom He has given EVERYTHING has responded to that gift in a most unexpected and glorious way—by giving EVERYTHING back to the Father. From the Son's perspective, the revelation of the Father's love and goodness was such that He could think of nothing else. From the Father's perspective, this return of glory comes with the greatest possible surprise and delight.

The Father, swelling with growing joy and pride in His begotten Son, once again gives Him EVERYTHING. And yet, somehow now the EVERYTHING that was before has increased.

How is it possible for the glory of God to increase? And yet, somehow His infinite joy is growing!

The Son cannot believe that the Father has once again given Him ALL. And this time, the ALL is more than before. Once again, He does not count equality with God as something to be held onto, so He empties Himself to the Father.

The Father in turn gives all of Himself to the Son.

The Glory, the Love, the Substantial Reality, the Name that is moving back and forth from Father to Son and from Son to Father is now constantly in motion. Holy Spirit runs back and forth, back and forth between Father and Son, like an electron's motion in an atom.

To an observer, He might appear like a cloud of glory surrounding them, constantly animating and filling the divine life. This bond of union, this glorious Spirit that unites them is so substantial, so real, so alive that He himself is personal, distinct, and yet completely united to Father and Son. He proceeds from the Father to the Son,[11] and then the Son returns Him to the Father. He is ever in motion, ever in between, ever burning with glory, life, power, knowledge, and beauty as He runs back and forth, back and forth in the divine song. The humility of the Spirit is to constantly help and serve the Father and Son. He is the secret of divine union, the Spirit who makes them one. He is glory Himself, yet He never seeks glory for Himself.

This dynamo of divine life has always been—there was never a time when it began. And yet, at a certain point, a decision was made for the ever-increasing divine joy and love to overflow into creation.

The plan was simple: Let's bring others into the song. Let us make man in our image. Let them join us in moving from glory to glory.

Let them be one as we are one.

How God is One

When we speak about the oneness of God, this is what that oneness looks like.

It is a dynamic union of Generosity (from the Father) and Gratitude (from the Son) mediated by the Spirit. We should think of this union as continual and constant—the Spirit is always in motion between the Father and the Son, back and forth, back and forth. The Spirit is the perfect bond of union between Father and Son.

If we could watch this dynamic in real time, we would see an incredibly beautiful, overwhelmingly glorious exchange of love back and forth. In the presence of this dynamic, we would feel enfolded and surrounded by a love that is so strong we would feel like we would die,

---

11 John 15:26: "When the Helper comes, whom I will send to you from the Father, that is the Spirit of truth who proceeds from the Father, He will testify about me."

and not care because it is so good. The sound of their song exceeds our most beautiful music by ten thousand times ten thousand.

The Father is both the conductor and the first violin in the song. He is the initiator, the first, the ultimate source of all power and authority. His first movement is to beget the Son, bestowing all He has on another.

The Son is the image of the invisible God, the one in whom all the fullness of God lives and dwells. He moves in response to the Father and returns all glory to the Father.

The Spirit is the one who proceeds from the Father. He is always traveling back and forth between the Father and the Son. He is the Helper of their union. He is the Name, the Truth, the Life, the Glory, the Goodness, the Love of God.

Life Through Death

This cycle not only maintains the glory and goodness of God. Paradoxically, it causes things to keep getting better and better.

At the extreme end of the cycle for both Father and Son, where they send forth the Spirit to the other, trusting their entire nature and being to the other person, where they "empty themselves," we find a situation analogous to night, sleep, and natural death.

Thus, when Jesus says "unless a grain of wheat dies it remains alone," He is not only using a natural analogy, He is unveiling an eternal truth. Increase in life can only come when one person completely gives themselves to the other in a radical act of faith. To breathe in, you must breathe out. To be exalted, you must humble yourself. To truly live, you must lay down your life. These are not just clever sayings of Jesus. This is the way of God's inner life. It's the only way of life He has ever known.

The joy of increase is only possible if we are willing to lay down our lives for one another!

Faith, Hope, and Love

And now, we can begin to see how Faith, Hope, and Love are all that remain eternally, for they are at the center of the music of God's inner life (1 Cor. 13).

Faith: The Father must trust all of Himself to the Son, and the Son must trust all of Himself to the Father. They both risk everything for one another. At any point, the other could refuse to "return glory." And yet, Father and Son continue to entrust themselves entirely to one another and will continue to do so forever.[12]

Hope: Although God is already infinitely glorious, paradoxically there is an increasing glory that comes with each exchange of glory. As Father and Son lay down their lives for one another, they move from glory to greater glory. This is not a closed system but a rapidly expanding realm of power and love that is oriented toward a better future.[13] Somehow, God's reality keeps getting better and better. Eternal Life,[14] or "knowing the Father and Son" is overflowing, abundant life that keeps getting better and better.

Love: Love is the beginning. When the Father gives His fullness to the Son, that is the essence of Love. Love is also the end goal. Love

---

12 John Wimber, founder of the Vineyard movement, famously said, "Faith is spelled R-I-S-K." As we can see, that statement is not only a clever and accurate description of our faith in God. It is an eternal truth.

13 As an aside here, the philosophical idea that God is somehow "outside of time" put forth by Augustine and many others is not dynamic enough to account for the living God of the Bible. This idea is better suited to the static, prime mover of Greek speculation. Instead, we ought to see time as flowing out of the inner life of God. This is made clear by the fact that Hope, with its future orientation, is an eternal part of His inner life. While God is certainly not bounded by our experience of time (He knows the end from the beginning) that does not mean God's inner experience is somehow static or frozen. Our experience of time as creatures no doubt originates in His inner life.

14 John 17:3

is most essentially the generous giving up of one's life for the other, the breathing out of the Spirit into the other, and then receiving the Spirit from the other in return as a fresh gift.

Faith, Hope, and Love endure forever. And love never fails. It is the secret of God's inner life.

The Glory Exchange

The Cross opens our ears to the music of God's inner life.

Now, when we read the prayer of Jesus in John 17:1, "Father… glorify your Son that the Son may glorify you…" we have some idea what He is requesting, what beauty and encounter He is longing to experience once again.

We can understand why the Son desired to become a man, to give everything back to the Father. His incarnation and crucifixion are an expression in history of the love they have eternally had for one another.

Now, when we read "Let them be one as we are one," we have some idea of what our Lord is praying for us.

He is praying for human beings to be caught up in the music of God's inner life. He wants us to come into the holy of holies, to be included in the inner circle of the life of the Trinity.

He is initiating us into this circle the same way His Father initiated Him: by giving everything He has for us, by laying down His life.

He knows that if He gives everything, goes lower than low, His Father will speak Him forth[15] once again, as He did in the beginning before the beginning. And when He emerges from death, the firstborn of a new creation, He is going to share His glory with us. He is going to give us the Holy Spirit. The secret bond of union between Father and Son will now unite men and women to God and to one another.

---

15 John 1:1-2

7

Into the Song

On November 21, 2009, I experienced three powerful visions from the Lord, back-to-back. These were visions that I saw in my mind's eye. More powerful than what I saw was the experience of the love of God that accompanied them—an intensity of love, pleasure, and joy that washed over me in waves, and left me physically exhausted after it passed.

I knew that all three of these visions connected to our kingly identity in Christ. These visions opened my eyes to spiritual realities that were always present in the Scriptures.[1] Meditation on these experiences and the Scriptures that correspond to them has informed the first section of this book.

The First Vision: Kingly Posture

In the first vision, I saw myself walking, surrounded on all sides by golden-hued bubble or ball that followed me wherever I went. As

---

[1] Personal prophetic experiences on their own are not a good foundation for doctrine. However, when these experiences are genuinely from God, they will agree with Scripture and are an incredible aid to understand the Scriptures. As Jesus says, "when the Helper comes…He will teach you all things and bring to your remembrance all things I said to you." As an evangelical, my first question to the Lord when I have a prophetic experiences is usually "Holy Spirit, can you show me where that is in the Bible?" I think it will be clear to the reader that these experiences line up quite powerfully with God's Word.

I walked, my arms never moved, yet everything around me fell into alignment and became as it was meant to be. Life grew at my feet as I walked forward. Ahead of me was dead ground, devoid of life, rocky and in stark black and white, void of color. But behind me was color, plant and animal life, deep green grass, water, and abundance.

I had a look of joy-filled bliss on my face, and my eyes were directed upward to heaven. My countenance was radiant, shining with glory.

As I saw these things, my natural body was rocked by wave after wave of the love of God, intensely powerful and enjoyable.

After the vision, I heard three phrases:

"Regal inactivity"

"Kingly posture"

"Ruling, not acting as a slave."

I knew the Lord was showing me how Jesus had walked on the earth, full of revelation of the love of heaven, and was inviting me to walk as He had walked. He was showing me what it meant to cease from my own works (my hands did nothing) and enter into His work as a king. It was evident how much more fruitful it would be to work with Him as a king.

The Second Vision: Lower Still

After the first vision ended, the waves of love subsided for a brief time, before becoming more intense than before. As these waves of love increased, I had a second vision.

In the vision, I was before the throne of God in Heaven. I saw Jesus standing before me in all His beauty. The only word I could think was "beauty." It was the most glorious thing I had ever seen and my body was washed with waves of His glory as I saw Him.

Chapter 7: Into the Song

I was so moved by the revelation of His beauty that I fell on my face on the ground before Him. However, the ground was not low enough, and I found myself attempting to go low, lower, and lower still. I was literally groveling on the floor, trying to claw my way through the floor, attempting in any way I could to go lower before Him. And this is why: the lower I went the more I was filled with every kind of delight—the lower I went, the more the love, pleasure, joy, and glory increased. The experience of the love of God was much greater than it had been in the first vision and kept increasing the lower I went.

Suddenly, a cry came out of my heart that my mind did not understand: "Lord, let me serve you."

My mind found this strange as I had somehow separated "love" and "service" in my mind.

However, this was a mere fleeting thought, a distraction. I continued to pour out my heart to the Lord, "I will gladly do the basest form of service for the privilege of being part of Your House. In fact, the lower, the more forgotten, abased, abused, overlooked, unimportant, reproached, despised, rejected, the more tortured the service, the BETTER."

My heart was utterly demolished as wave after wave of love washed over me, causing my body to physically shake.

From this lowly position on my face, I saw His hands catch mine. He raised me up by the hand from my blissful, prostrate position.

I saw my body pass through His, as if we were superimposed on one another, and I knew He was imparting a kind of equality to me, raising me up to His image, and also imparting His identity. My mind was scandalized, "How can Jesus be sharing this with me?" But I was too overwhelmed by love to protest. The waves of love, pleasure, and delight kept washing over me. I was undone.

The Third Vision: Seated with Him

After another intermission, I began to feel the waves of love increase.

"Hang on," I found myself thinking, knowing the encounter was about to increase.

In this final vision, I saw Jesus again, but this time not in all His beauty, but as my glorious Friend.

He looked into my eyes with a radiant face, smiling. In this vision, unlike the last one, I had the ability to stand up, although in my actual physical body, I fell down anyway before Him, imitating the previous experience. But this was not what He wanted this time. Right away, He raised me up by the hand and gazed at me, eye to eye, with golden, blazing love. I felt as He gazed into my eyes, He was once again imparting a kind of equality to me.

As He gazed at me, He placed a crown on my head. The crown was weighty with glory, and my neck had a hard time holding it up. My conscious mind again broke in with bad advice, "I should be casting this at His feet," I thought. But, one look from Him and I understood I was not to do that right now. I was to keep the crown on my head.

Next, I looked down and saw a scepter in my right hand. He told me to sit down on His throne, which filled me with concern. Despite this, I obeyed and sat down on His throne with Him. Once again, our bodies were superimposed on one another as in the second vision. I was in Him and He was in me.

As I sat, I found I was back in the heavenly throne room, but viewed it from His perspective, seeing the worshippers facing Him (they were not worshipping me, but I was seated where He was—my mind was very concerned about this).

I didn't know what to do, but I knew He wanted me to do something kingly, to exercise authority. I just didn't know what to do.

Instinctively I raised both hands, including the scepter in my right hand, and motioned to the sides, like a conductor directing an orchestra.

When I did this, the back of the room parted in half, revealing an enormous tsunami of water crashing through the throne room, crashing through the worshippers, and crashing into me where I was seated on the throne. While this may sound terrifying, I was unafraid of the tsunami. When it hit me, I was filled with a massive wave of the love and pleasure of God.

As the giant wave hit me, I heard the words "Lord over the Flood," a reference to Psalm 29:10: "The LORD sits enthroned above the flood. The LORD sits enthroned as king forever."

The Aftermath

After these experiences ended, I was completely exhausted. While I had other work to accomplish that day, I was unable to do anything else. My mind and body had been overloaded by the love of God. When I shared about my encounter with a close friend who is an Anglican priest, he informed me that I had these experiences on the day before "Christ the King" Sunday on the Church Calendar. It is the last feast of the Church year, coming the Sunday before the new year begins with Advent, a feast celebrating the soon return of Jesus Christ.

Three Aspects of Jesus's Ministry

As I pondered these things in my heart, I began to understand some aspects of the three visions. I began to see how each vision related to a different period of Jesus's ministry. The Lord was inviting me to be part of all three.

In the first vision, I saw myself walking on earth as Jesus had walked on earth, as a kingly ambassador from a glorious Kingdom, bringing the life of that Kingdom everywhere He went. Before the cross, Jesus constantly went around doing good and expressing the power and love of the Father on earth. I knew this first vision corresponded to Jesus's earthly ministry of preaching, healing, and deliverance.

In the second vision, the revelation of the beauty of Jesus compelled me to ask to serve Him in the lowest way imaginable. I knew this experience spoke to the Lord's death on the cross.

In the third vision, the Lord invited me to sit on His throne with Him and do "king stuff." I didn't know what that meant, but when I raised up my hands, it released a flood of His glory. In the book of Acts, just ten days after Jesus ascends to Heaven and sits at God's right hand, the Holy Spirit is poured out. I knew this vision corresponded to His ascended ministry.

Equality with Christ

In all these visions, I was scandalized by how much the Lord was imparting equality with Himself to me. While my Spirit came alive when He did these things, my mind was embarrassed. I felt the way I imagine my dog would feel if I ever invited her to sleep in my bed (she is a good dog and knows this is not allowed).[2] My mind was screaming, "Lord, you are the Lord! You can't share your very nature with me like this. You can't share your throne like this." And yet, He was sharing it.[3]

If these were just someone's visions, we might easily dismiss these claims as delusional and heretical. Yet, as we have seen, this is precisely the invitation Jesus extends to us in many Scriptures, and especially in John 17. He is bringing us into God's inner life as full participants.

---

2   No judgement implied to those who allow dogs or cats in their beds. Your pets are more blessed than mine.

3   Revelation 3:21 (and many other passages in Revelation) speaks of this as a future reality. Ephesians 2:6 speaks of the present aspect of this reality.

This is what the gift of the Spirit means. Just as His Father bestowed equality on Him, while retaining His ultimate authority, now Christ has done the same for us. He is not only our Lord, but also our brother.[4]

Seeing His Beauty

The second vision was by far the most powerful and most intense of the three.

The eyes of my heart were opened to see Jesus in His glory and it was devastatingly beautiful. I could think of nothing, nothing but finding a way to go lower before Him, to give all my being away ten thousand times to serve Him. The unquenchable desire to go lower, lower, and lower in the presence of His beauty was all I could think about. I finally understood why the twenty-four elders cast their crowns before the throne.[5] I assure you, it is not a gentle toss—they are hurling the crowns with all their might, ripping them from their heads in utter abandon, longing to go low, lower, lower still, constantly undone by the beauty of the one who sits on the throne.

In that moment, I also understood why Jesus chose to become a man and go to the cross. In the full light of the Father's beauty before the foundation of the world, He was filled with the same desire. No low was low enough for the Son in light of the Father's glory. And, on the other side of the cross, no high was high enough for the Father to exalt Him.[6]

These are great mysteries in Scripture. My eyes had been opened.

Since that time, in moments of intense suffering, I have thought

---

4　John 20:17 "Do not cling to me, for I have not yet ascended to the Father; but go to my brothers and say to them, 'I am ascending to my Father and your Father, to my God and your God.'"
5　Revelation 4
6　Philippians 2:9-10 and many others

about what I prayed—to go low, lower, lower still. One time in particular, as I was in agony and questioning how God was treating me, He asked me: "You told me you wanted to serve me, and the lower, the more forgotten, abased, abused, overlooked, unimportant, reproached, despised, rejected, the more tortured the service, the better. Do you still feel that way, or do you want to take it back?"

It's never wise to walk away from moments of revelation and faith in moments of pain, confusion, and doubt. I realized He was giving me the treasure I had requested out of revelation of His beauty. I decided to stay the course.

The Ascended Reality

In the third vision, I saw how Jesus wanted me, and us as His people, to partake of His ascended reality even now. Paul describes this in Ephesians 2:6, "…and raised us up together and made us sit together in the heavenly places in Christ Jesus." He wants to extend equality to us as His brothers, to partner with us in extending His royal scepter and releasing a flood of His glory that will cover the earth, the great outpouring at the end of the age.

Welcomed into the Song

Jesus prayed, "Let them be one, just as we are one."

In 2,000 years, we have not seen this prayer answered in fullness. And yet, Jesus gets what He prays for.

The Father is going to answer Jesus's prayer. He has already begun to answer the prayer, starting in Acts 2 on the day of Pentecost with the gift of the Holy Spirit. The Father has constantly been moving throughout history to answer Jesus's prayer. He is very wise, very strategic, and incredibly patient. The Holy Spirit is the key member of the Trinity charged with implementing the Father's plan. He is the bond of union between Father and Son. He is the Name, the Truth, the Glory, and the Love of the Father that make us one. He will not relent until we are perfectly united with the Lord and with one another.

A generation is coming that will walk in John 17 unity as their new normal.

Powered flight was impossible for all human history. Today, flying is completely normal. It will be the same way with Jesus's prayer in John 17. It seems impossible today, but for a future generation, it will be normal Christianity. Once it is normal, everyone who wants to will be able to fly.

The generation that sees John 17 answered will fully accept Jesus's invitation into the song of God's inner life. He has abundantly provided for us by His own blood and by the gift of the Spirit. They will take the united life of God in heaven, the song revealed in these three visions, the inner life of Father, Son, and Spirit revealed in John 17 and throughout the New Testament, and live it out together on earth. What was once impossible will be impossible to hide.

They will be perfectly one, "…so that the world will know that you sent me and have loved them just as you have loved me."

Part 2: Same Game, Different Seats

Do other parts of Scripture foresee a glorious, united church?
What historical precedents might prepare us for such a revolution?
What might the fulfillment of John 17 look like?

1

Until Unity

It's a hot, muggy summer day and I'm on my way to the ballpark, fifty dollars burning a hole in my pocket. I approach the stadium, holding my young daughter's hand, guiding her through the excited, rowdy crowd with an ear raised, listening.

Then I hear it:

"Tiiiickets."

I've found my scalper.

The negotiations begin. He wants to sell me two tickets for $100. Their face value is $140. I'm assured that it's a very good deal and they're very good seats.

I explain my predicament: I only have fifty dollars cash. I'm also happy to just go to the ticket counter and get cheap seats for twenty bucks. He raises his voice. I match his energy. Just as I begin to walk away, he relents. Apparently, I look like a guy who only has fifty dollars.

We have our seats, somewhere lower down on the third base side. I'm excited. I've never seen a game from these seats before.

I love getting tickets from scalpers because you never know what seat you will get. Every seat means seeing the game from a new perspective. If you're sitting close in, you're immersed in the action, the humanity of the players. You understand the speed of a fastball viscerally. You can hear what the players are saying each other, and to the umpires. If you're seated higher up and behind home plate, you're sitting where the announcers sit. From there, you have a "God's eye" view of the game from above. If you're in the outfield bleachers, you might catch a home run ball. If you're watching from your couch at home, you're getting a custom mix of many camera angles, many perspectives, another version of the "God's eye" view. At home, you're missing the smell and feel of the whole ballpark but it's comfortable and you have the play-by-play of the announcers interpreting the game for you.

Perspective at the game isn't just a matter of where you're sitting. It's affected by why you're there. Are you cheering for the home team, or the visitors? Are you there to watch baseball, to eat and drink, or to spend time with your friends? All these motivations affect what we see at the game.

There's one game happening, but there are many perspectives on the game. The same reality is present, viewed by all—but the different perspectives cause us to notice different things, things we couldn't see from another seat. And, if you're at the ballpark, your presence adds to the richness of the experience for everyone else. You're part of the story. As we saw in 2020, baseball without fans is not the same.

Different Perspectives on John 17 Unity

In seminary, I learned a basic principle of biblical interpretation: Don't build an entire theology around one verse.

It's easy to get laser-focused on one Bible passage that says something we like and forget about other passages that bring a different perspective. When the counsel of Scripture is taken as a whole, we get a better sense of what God is really saying.

If the Father is planning to answer Jesus's prayer, it is a very big deal. If it is part of God's overall plan, we would expect to hear the themes of John 17 echoed throughout the Bible, from Genesis to Revelation. If "the game" is a Church that becomes "one as we are one" before the Lord returns, we should be able to see what Jesus is praying for from different seats in the stadium. Furthermore, those seats should enrich our understanding of Jesus's prayer, adding perspective we don't get from John 17 itself.

Now that we have a thorough understanding of Jesus's prayer, we are going to search the Scriptures through this lens.

John 17 predicts a revolutionary change in the church, a change so dramatic and different from our current situation, it is difficult to even imagine. In addition to Scripture, we will examine spiritual and secular history in search of precedents and pitfalls for potential revolutionaries. Finally, we will explore imaginatively based on God's word what a fulfillment of John 17 could look like.

Ephesians 4: Present and Future Unity

The book of Ephesians is unique among the Pauline epistles. It doesn't seem to have been written to address a particular problem, unlike 1 Corinthians (divisions and immorality) or Galatians (a false gospel) but rather for Paul to give a clear statement of the gospel message. Ephesians gives us a "God's eye" view of where the church is headed. At many moments in the letter, Paul seems transported into heavenly places as he beholds the wonder of God's plan for the church.

The Wonderful Reality of Present Unity

In Ephesians chapter 4, Paul speaks about unity in the church.

"Therefore I, the prisoner of the Lord, urge you to walk

> in a manner worthy of the calling with which you have been called, with all humility and gentleness, with patience, bearing with one another in love, being diligent to maintain [keep, guard] the unity of the Spirit in the bond of peace. There is one body and one Spirit, just as you also were called in one hope of your calling; one Lord, one faith, one baptism, one God and Father of all who is over all and through all and in all." Eph. 4:1-6

Paul acknowledges a fundamental unity among believers that already exists, a unity that we must work to maintain. This unity comes from the present gift of the Holy Spirit; it is called "the unity of the Spirit."

Notice how Trinitarian the present unity is, involving Father, Son, and Spirit.

> "There is one body and one Spirit, just as you also were called in one hope of your calling; one Lord [Jesus Christ], one faith, one baptism, one God and Father of all who is over all and through all and in all." Ephesians 4:4-6

Through the gift of the Spirit that has already come, true believers in Jesus Christ are already experiencing an incredible union with one another.

Why are We a Body?

Paul repeatedly calls believers "a body" and "the body of Christ." It is a powerful idea that can become obscured by common usage. What makes believers in Jesus the body of Christ? Quite simply, we are the body of Christ because we have the Spirit of Christ in us.

A spirit is what animates and inhabits a living being. Using just my mind, my thinking, or my emotions, I cannot move a rock, a tree, or a table. My personal spirit is not in the rock. When I strike the rock, I feel no pain from the rock. It is not part of my body. However, I can move my hands and feet. I can move my legs, my mouth, and my head. When the rock hits my hand, I feel pain in my hand. These are all parts of my body. My body is everywhere my spirit can move, or to put it another way, everything I can affect just by thinking. My body is my "inner world" through which I interact with an "outer world" of objects I cannot affect with my mind.

The Spirit of Christ inhabits the church in the same way our personal spirit inhabits our body. Truly, "we have the mind of Christ."[1] We are not metaphorically the body of Christ. We are His Body in a literal sense—His Spirit inhabits us. We are His inner world. Because His Spirit dwells in us together, believers in Christ are already parts of one another in an intimate, ontological way. If we have the Holy Spirit in us, we are already "one being with many persons"[2] just as my own body is one being with many parts, united by my personal spirit.

As we've focused on the future fullness of John 17 unity, it would be easy to gloss over the powerful unity that exists through the Spirit right now, a union the Ephesian church also experienced. I've met believers from around the world. Despite the barriers of culture, there is an instant connection that comes about by the working of the Holy Spirit, an unusual degree of love for one another. This current level of unity is precious. Paul urges us to diligently guard it and maintain it.

However, Paul does not anticipate that the current level of unity will simply be maintained indefinitely. He sees the church of his day like a small child that is already "one" but will grow and express deeper unity as it matures. The current level of unity is just the beginning. He sees something higher and greater on the horizon.

---

1 1 Corinthians 2
2 As God is in the Nicene Creed and other definitions of the Trinity. This is the unbelievable power of the indwelling Spirit.

Mature Unity

Ephesians 4:7-13 gives specific insight into how the Church will grow up into greater unity:

> "But to each one of us grace was given according to the measure of Christ's gift. Therefore it says,
>
> > 'When He ascended on high,
> > He led captive *the* captives,
> > And He gave gifts to people.'
>
> (Now this expression, 'He ascended,' what does it mean except that He also had descended into the lower parts of the earth? He who descended is Himself also He who ascended far above all the heavens, so that He might fill all things.) And He gave some as apostles, some as prophets, some as evangelists, some as pastors and teachers, for the equipping of the saints for the work of ministry, for the building up of the body of Christ..."

In verse 7, we see that God has distributed His grace gifts throughout His body through the Holy Spirit. This is important: God's plan to help us grow up corporately is dependent on the grace He has given *to other human beings*. There are certain gifts of God we can only get from other people in the church—He won't give them to us directly. God has hidden what you need to grow in other people. Likewise, the grace given to you is essential to the spiritual life and well being of others. God has done this so that we are dependent on one another in the same way the members of the Trinity are dependent on one another.

In this passage, Paul describes how the Father has given five different kinds of leadership gifts, Apostles, Prophets, Evangelists, Pastors, and Teachers, to equip every member of the body of Christ to use their own grace gifts and serve one another in a harmonious way.

The process looks like this: We gratefully guard and maintain the unity we already have. God sends us various types of leadership to equip us to serve one another, which in turn builds up the Body in love, causing the love and unity to grow and increase. The initial unity we were preserving is now stronger and richer than before.

This growth process continues and repeats, like a tree putting on annual rings, but the growth is not forever; it has an end-goal. Paul describes the ultimate goal in Ephesians 4:13:

> "until we all attain to the unity of the faith, and of
> the knowledge of the Son of God, to a mature man, to
> the measure of the stature which belongs to the fullness
> of Christ."

Paul sees the same end-goal for the people of God that Jesus sees—a body of believers built up through love and the grace of God until they are completely one. When we hear Paul saying, "until we all reach the unity of the faith," we should hear Jesus saying, "Let them be one as we are one."

Paul and Jesus may be sitting in different seats and using different language but they're watching the same game. Ephesians 4:13 and John 17:23 are both describing the future, glorious state of the church before the Lord returns.

New Ways to Speak about Unity

One of the most common biblical literary devices is to repeat the same idea in a slightly different way.

Consider this from the Psalm 1:1:

> "Blessed is the man who does not walk in the counsel of
> the wicked,
> Nor stand in the path of sinners,
> Nor sit in the seat of scoffers!"

You'll notice that "wicked, sinners, and scoffers" are all parallel. So are "walk, stand, and sit" and "counsel, path, and seat." The Psalmist is communicating the same idea in a slightly different way three different times. The result is like binocular vision, or trinocular in this example—we see the same reality from slightly different perspectives, adding a greater fullness to what we see.

While the gospel of John gives us the phrases "let them be one as we are one" and "perfected in unity," Paul describes ultimate oneness in four new ways. His new perspective gives us a more complete view of what perfect unity will look like:

"Until we all reach the unity of the faith…"
"…and [unity of] knowledge of the Son of God…"
"…To a mature man…"
"…To the measure of the stature of the fullness of Christ…"

He foresees a future state of the church where we reach a level of unity in faith and the knowledge of Christ Jesus that has not yet been seen. He sees this future united state as the equivalent of physical maturity in a man, and says we will reach "the measure of the stature of the fullness of Christ." He uses the powerful word "fullness," a word that is so important in understanding the glory exchange between Father and Son, to describe this future, united church.

While throughout history, many have striven for personal maturity—a worthy goal—it should be clear that what Paul is describing here is a corporate reality. We cannot achieve it by becoming individually mature. This is describing the corporate church in one moment of time, one generation.

In contrast to this corporate maturity, He describes a corporate childishness in verse 14, one where believers are easily tossed about by false doctrine, deceit, and trickery. While this childish state may have described the Ephesian church at that time, Paul wanted them to aim to grow up. Returning to the body paradigm, Paul envisions a church where the whole body is proportional and integrated with its mature head, Christ Jesus (Eph. 4:15-16).

Ephesians 4 and John 17

While the key word "unity" may be our first clue that Paul is describing the same future reality that Jesus prayed for in John 17, it's far from the only confirmation. Incredibly, Paul sees the church looking quite divine, having the "measure of the stature of the fullness of Christ." This is just like John 17 where we see the people of God partaking of divine attributes.

Both Ephesians 4 and John 17 describe the future, glorious state of the church prior to the Lord's return. Paul shares this mystery with the Ephesians as something to strive for and live up to. Paul's new perspective gives us new language, a new way to view what is going to happen. This future state is not only "one as we are one." It can also be called "maturity," "the measure of the stature of the fullness of Christ," "unity of the knowledge of the Son of God," and "the unity of the faith."

All of these concepts overlap and refer to the same end-state of the church prior to the return of the Lord Jesus. All these phrases are different ways of describing the same reality Jesus is praying for in John 17. It's the same game from different seats.

Unity is Corporate Holiness

Ephesians 5:22-33 presents itself on the surface as basic advice for a happy marriage. Wives should follow the leadership of their husbands, and husbands should love and sacrificially care for their wives.

However, this passage is not primarily about natural marriages—

it's mostly about what is happening between Christ and His Church. Paul, as he has been throughout the book of Ephesians, is caught up in rapture envisioning the future, glorious state of the Church. We'll pick up the drama in v. 25:

> "Husbands, love your wives just as Christ loved the church and gave Himself for her, that He might sanctify and cleanse her by the washing of water by the word, that *He might present her to Himself a glorious church, not having spot or wrinkle or any such thing, but that she should be holy and without blemish.*"

Once again, we begin to hear echoes of John 17. Paul describes a holy church, sanctified and washed clean by the Word of God (John 17:15-19), that is full of glory (John 17:22) and without spot or blemish (John 17:17). Paul is describing the same "mature unity" of Ephesians 4:13 using the paradigm of marriage and the "bride of Christ" instead of the "body of Christ."

The body paradigm focuses on how we have the Spirit of Christ inside us, and therefore are parts of His body. While we are Christ's body already, because we already have the Spirit, someday we will be fully grown and mature. This is what Ephesians 4 and John 17 prophesy.

We are also Christ's body in another way, although this is prospective, not realized at this time. Just as the wife is an extension of the husband's body and the husband an extension of his wife's,[3] so the Church is to be married to Jesus and experience a much greater degree of union than we currently experience in this age.

Just as the first Adam rejoiced over Eve and said "this is bone of my bone, and flesh of my flesh," so Jesus Christ, the second Adam rejoices over us. We are His flesh and His bone—His eternal companion. When He slept the sleep of death, the Father brought us forth from

---

3   Referencing Genesis 2 here along with Paul.

His wounded side, to be His bride. When He awoke, He saw the desire of His heart. Until the day of consummation at the end of this age, He is serving us, washing us, speaking His word to us, cleansing us to present us to Himself pure, spotless, and glorious.

Unity, in this sense, is corporate holiness or purity. And corporate holiness is nothing less than preparation for the greatest wedding party in history, the culmination of the ages when the Bride is finally made ready for her Husband, when the marriage of heaven and earth is finally consummated.

Unity and the End of the Age

If our understanding of Ephesians 4 and 5 is correct, that the emergence of a glorious, mature, and united church is closely connected to the end of the age, we would expect to hear about it in the book of Revelation.

Revelation 19:7-8 describes the time immediately before the Lord Jesus returns to earth. During the greatest period of evil in human history, even as the righteous judgements of God are being poured out, we hear this song breaking through:

> "Let us be glad and rejoice and give Him glory, for the marriage of the Lamb has come, and His wife has made herself ready. And to her it was granted to be arrayed in fine linen, for the fine linen is the righteous acts of the saints."

Ephesians 5 and Revelation 19 are looking into the same reality: the wife of the Lamb, the bride of Christ, is characterized by readiness, holiness, and righteousness. She is without spot or wrinkle, clothed in spotless linen. The bride is mature, prepared, and righteous at the time of the Lord's return. John the apostle, in his later days, is seeing the end goal Jesus prayed for as he leaned upon His chest as a young man.

Now, as we approach the wedding of the ages, Christ in heaven, through the ministry of the Spirit, is bringing His bride to a place of glorious purity and holiness by the washing of the Word of God that removes every spot, wrinkle, and blemish.

Paul and John both foresee a glorious future for the church in advance of this wedding. This future of unmatched purity and holiness is the same state Jesus prays for in John 17, "let them be perfectly [completely] one."

Unity is nothing other than corporate holiness. No wonder it is the work of the Holy Spirit.

Same Game, Different Seats

John 17, Ephesians 4 and 5, Revelation 19. It is clear these biblical authors, led by the Holy Spirit, are watching the same game from different seats. They're gazing into the future using slightly different language to describe the same reality. They are longing with prophetic anticipation for a glorious, holy, united, mature Church prior to the return of Jesus.

By noticing they are speaking of the same reality, we receive a fuller vision of what mature unity will look like. Ephesians and Revelation gift us an expanded language that speaks of this future, glorious church, opening up our eyes to notice when other scriptures speak about this topic.

From now on, when the Scriptures speak about fullness, corporate maturity, holiness, purity, the knowledge of Christ, mature righteousness, a wedding, and perfected unity or oneness, our ears should perk up. The reality Jesus prayed for in John 17 is likely being discussed.

2

The Roadmap

I never met my wife's grandmother in person before she died, but my conversations with her on the phone were unforgettable. "Yiayia" was born in Greece before immigrating to the States as a young woman. She spoke with a thick Greek accent and never fully mastered English grammar.

"I want to speak to the Cassiani," she would tell me, using my wife's full Greek name. Adding a definite article to a proper name is required in Greek, but it sounds very strange in English. She'd also mix up the order of words. Once again, Greek grammar has different rules, and words can be placed in a more flexible order than in English. In one memorable and hilarious voicemail, she plaintively asked, "Talk me, I want to call to you."

While Cassi and I had a little bit of fun with her grammatical errors, there is no doubt she had the last laugh. I was studying ancient Greek at the time, and when she asked me to say something to her in Greek, I read a bit of John's gospel to her right off the page.

Silence greeted me on the other side of the line. After an exaggerated pause, she said, "I want to speak to the Cassiani."

She informed my wife in no uncertain terms that the words I had spoken bore no resemblance to Greek, ancient or modern.

Those who speak a language fluently rarely think about grammar. They simply speak. They embody the grammar effortlessly. However, those who are learning a language need to pay close attention to grammar until it becomes second nature. The grammar of the language is the pattern of the language.

Similarly, most people do not consult roadmaps or GPS for their daily commute. However, when you're driving somewhere new, having a map or clear directions is essential.

In terms of divine unity, none of us are fluent. We all sound like Yiayia speaking English, or me trying to speak Greek. All of us are learning a new language—a heavenly language. In fact, we are learning the original language; the language of God's inner life. We are going to the most ancient place imaginable, but for us it is new, a place we have never been before.

We need to learn divine grammar. We need to see that pattern that leads to John 17. We need a map to show us how to bring God's inner life to earth.

The Divine Mindset

In Philippians 2:1-11, Paul gives just that: a step-by-step map to being of one mind and heart. If we follow the directions, we will find ourselves walking in ever increasing unity with one another. The "map" portion begins in verses 5-11. Let's pick up the narrative in verse 2, where he makes his goal clear:

> "Complete my joy by being of the same mind, having the same love, being in full accord and of one mind."

His goal is the unity of the believers in Philippi, which he says will complete, or fulfill his joy. This phrase calls to mind Jesus's words in John 15:11. He also commands love for one another so that "my joy may be in you and your joy may be complete."

In verses 3-4 he warns them about a dangerous pitfall:

> "Do nothing from selfish ambition or conceit, but in humility count others more significant than yourselves. Let each of you look not only to his own interests but also to the interests of others."

Divine unity is incompatible with selfish ambition. In fact, it requires us to honor one another above ourselves and consider their interests (at times) even higher than our own. As James 3:14-16 warns us:

> "But if you harbor bitter envy and selfish ambition in your hearts, do not boast about it or deny the truth. Such 'wisdom' does not come down from heaven but is earthly, unspiritual, demonic. For where you have envy and selfish ambition, there you find disorder and every evil thing."

Conceit, envy, jealousy of others, and selfish ambition have a demonic type of wisdom to them, a wisdom that releases "every evil thing." No wonder Paul is cautioning believers against this trap of the enemy. Selfish ambition opens a portal to Hell itself.

With this warning ringing in our ears, in verses 5-11, he lays out the complete roadmap to mature unity. The roadmap for followers of Jesus is nothing more or less than the pattern of the life of Jesus Christ.

> "Let this mind be in you [followers of Jesus] that was also in Christ Jesus, who, being in the form of God did not count equality with God as something to be grasped, but emptied Himself, taking the form of a servant, and being found in the likeness of man, He humbled Himself, and became obedient unto death, even the death of the cross. Therefore, God also has highly exalted Him and given Him the name which is above every name

that at the name of Jesus every knee should bow in heaven and on earth, and under the earth, and every tongue confess that Jesus Christ is Lord to the glory of God the Father."

Notice how the roadmap begins at a high point, with Christ in Heaven, possessing equality with God. However, from that initial high point, we enter a precipitous descent. Jesus did not consider the equality He had with the Father as something to be clung to. Instead, He sacrificed everything He had received from the Father, moving low, lower, and lower still unto the point of death and even the lowest form of death, death on a cross.

At this lowest point, the Father can stand it no longer. He resurrects the Son, His perfect image, and exalts Him back to His right hand. Now, the Son is even higher than He was before He descended.[1] The Father gives Him the highest name, crowning Him Lord of all, commanding all of creation to worship Him.

As we have previously seen, the life of Jesus revealed the eternal inner life of God on earth. This was not a new way of thinking He adopted to redeem humanity. This is how Christ has always thought—it's the pattern of thinking He received from His Father. This is the mindset of the Trinity, the thoughts that produce divine union within the Godhead. If we want to be one as they are one, we must follow this map, we must learn the grammar of union. If we want to be one as they are one, we must learn to think like Christ.

A Second Map

Philippians 2 is not the only example of this map in Scripture. Remarkably, John 13:1-17, the beginning of Jesus's last supper discourse that culminates in John 17, lays out the same pattern. Here, the map is

---

[1] Higher because now He now possess all authority not only in heaven, but also on earth.

presented as a beautiful tableau. Jesus acts out a dramatized parable to show us the path to perfect love.

> "Jesus knew that the Father had put all things under his power, and that he had come from God and was returning to God; so he got up from the meal, took off his outer clothing, and wrapped a towel around his waist. After that, he poured water into a basin and began to wash his disciples' feet, drying them with the towel that was wrapped around him…When he had finished washing their feet, he put on his clothes and returned to his place." John 13:3-5, 12

In verse 3, Jesus begins seated at the head of the table. From this position, He recognizes that the Father has given Him all things, and that He has come from God and is going back to God. With this in full view, He stands up, removes his "royal" outer robes,[2] puts on a towel, stoops over, and begins to wash the feet of His disciples, taking on a role normally reserved for the lowest of servants.

After He has washed their feet, He stands up, removes the towel, puts on His robes again, and sits down again at the head of the table. It's a dramatized version of His entire ministry. It's the same pattern as Philippians 2.

After acting out His entire ministry symbolically, Jesus says:

"Do you understand what I have done for you?"

In the moment, His disciples had no clue.

> "You call Me Teacher and Lord, and you say well, for so I am. If I then, your Lord and Teacher have washed

---

2   Robes or outer clothing are here symbolic of glory. Clothing is often a symbol or indicator of honor in Scripture. Think of Genesis 3, when Adam and Eve realize they are naked as the first mention of this theme, or of Elijah's mantle that Elisha picks up as some well-known examples of this.

> your feet, you also ought to wash one another's feet. For I have given you an example [a pattern], that you should do as I have done…"

While His disciples at the time had no idea what He was doing or what it meant for them, they soon figured it out. And we must also understand what He has done for us.

Through the parable of the basin and the towel, Jesus reveals the pattern of God's inner life. For all of eternity, He has fully given His life to the Father, and again received His life from the Father. This exchange of glory is central to their life. In John 13, He enacts this eternal pattern once again, but this time instead of serving His Father—"washing His feet," as it were, He is serving His disciples. He is looping us into the inner life of God.

Can you see the unbelievable weight of what He has done? He is bringing human beings into God's inner circle, into His inner life.

> "…If you understand these things, you are blessed if you do them." John 13:17

It is possible for us to understand the scandal that Jesus is sharing the divine nature with human beings and yet still miss His main point: He is showing us how we must treat one another. He is looping us in so that we can loop one another into God's inner life. His sacrifice is not complete, His joy is not full until we love one another in the same way He loved us.

Both John 13 and Philippians 2 are clearly focused on how our actions toward other believers must match the pattern given to us by Jesus.

This is not only what He has done for us. This is not just how God acts with God. It must become the pattern of our lives together. And it's not enough just to understand the pattern. The blessing comes to those who do it.

The Map as a Commandment

Just a few verses later, in John 13:34-35, Jesus gives us the pattern in a new form.

He summarizes the pattern and gives it, like a second Moses descending from on high, as a New Commandment:

> "A new commandment I give to you, love one another, just as I have loved you, that you also love one another. By this all will know that you are My disciples, if you have love for one another."

Just as in Jesus's prayer, the comparison is doing all the work. To fulfill His new commandment, everything depends on knowing how Jesus has loved us. Only after we understand His love can we fulfill the second part of the command, to love one another in exactly the same way.

This commandment is similar to a major commandment from the Old Testament, "Love your neighbor as you love yourself." However, while they are similar, they are not the same. The New Commandment is completely new.

The comparisons make all the difference.

In the Old Covenant, the command is to "love your neighbor as yourself." The comparison depends on you: your love for yourself. In the New Covenant, the command is to "love one another as I have loved you." The comparison depends on Jesus. The way He loved us is the new standard for how we should love each other. The New Commandment could never exist without the pattern of Jesus's life, the map we see in Philippians 2 and John 13.

The Meaning of "One Another"

The New Commandment is to love "one another" as I have loved you. Who exactly is He commanding us to love?

A common mistake is to see the importance of the New Commandment and then assume it must be about loving God. But clearly, Jesus is not commanding love for God. In fact, He addresses this common error in John 14:15, "If you love Me, you will keep my commandments." In other words, if you want to express love for me, do what I commanded you, which is "love one another as I have loved you."[3]

The New Commandment is also not about loving "the world" or unbelievers. We know that God loves the unbelieving world so much that He sent His Son into the world. And we must love them as well. However, that is not what the New Commandment commands.

The New Commandment is not about loving God or loving unbelievers. It is about loving one another. It is about Christians loving other Christians.

The Divine Dance

The New Commandment only makes sense if we understand the pattern of how Jesus has loved us. We must see it and understand it. Then we copy what He did and walk out the pattern with other believers.

Jesus is showing us the divine dance, teaching us the moves that have united Father and Son for all eternity. He's inviting us into the dance. However, this dance is not a free-for-all. We can only join if we learn the right moves and follow the pattern He shows us.

This dance is difficult. It requires extreme trust, not only in God, but also in one another. It involves a complete self-giving of our power, our name, our nature, and our glory not only to God (although this is also true), but to one another.

---

[3] This is not to minimize other commands of Jesus, the Great Commission, for example. However, in context it is clear He is referring pre-eminently to the New Commandment.

The trust required for the dance seems foolish, risky, even irresponsible. There is no guarantee others will do their part as we hurl our bodies into the air, trusting them to catch us inches from the ground.

And yet, if we have been touched by His love, we can respond in no other way. We must love them as He has loved us. The love of Christ compels us.

Step-by-Step into the Dance

> "Love one another, just as I loved you, that you also love one another in the same way." John 13:34

> "Have this mind among you that was in Christ Jesus" Philippians 2:5

John 17 unity is the end-goal, our destination, but Jesus's New Commandment is how we get there. To put it another way, John 17 unity is the ultimate result of "loving one another as I have loved you," in the same way that arriving in Los Angeles from New York is the ultimate result of driving thousands of miles over many hours.

John 13:1-17 and Philippians 2:5-11 both show us the pattern of how Jesus loved us. We might say the New Commandment has these passages embedded within it, since they show us clearly and succinctly how Jesus loved us.

Because this heavenly dance is so new and foreign to us, and because the pattern is so essential to reach John 17 unity, we will map out each movement in detail, step-by-step.

Step 1: Object of Love

> "...knowing the Father had given all things into His hands, and that He had come forth from God, and was going back to God." John 13:3

"who, being in the form of God..." Philippians 2:6

To follow the pattern of Jesus, you first must know who you are.

Just as the Father shared His nature, His glory, His goodness with the Son, now the Son has shared His nature, His glory, and His goodness with us. Truly, if we are in Christ, from Him we have all received "grace upon grace" and we are "co-heirs" with Christ, inheritors of all things in heaven and on earth.[4] We are recipients of the Father's love in the same way Jesus is (John 17:23, 26).

Because of what Christ has done for us, we are now seated in the best seat in all the universe.[5] We cannot conceive of a position of greater blessedness than what we now enjoy as a free gift from Him, having done nothing to deserve it! To put it another way, our Father is unbelievably richer than we could ask, think, or imagine, and we get to enjoy that wealth for all of eternity.

This love is ours *positionally*. We understand by faith we have been given the best seat. The Bible tells us so. But, by the gift of the Holy Spirit, this love is also ours *experientially*. We have practical, tangible knowledge of the love of God, a down payment of what is forever ours, because the very Spirit of God lives in us.

If you want to walk like Jesus, you first have to know you are loved like Jesus.

Step 2: Lay Aside your Glory

"...rose from supper and laid down his mantle..." John 13:4

"...did not count equality with God as something to be grasped or clung to..." Phil. 2:6

---

4   Romans 8, Ephesians 1-2, John 1
5   Ephesians 2

We are God's beloved, co-heirs with the Messiah, possessing a type of equality with Jesus as brothers. We receive the Father's love just as He received it. However, as we experience the glory and beauty of God's love, it fills us with a seemingly contradictory desire: the overflowing desire of a ravished heart to give it all away.

Just as the Son was overwhelmed by the Father giving all things to Him and immediately moved to return thanks, so when we truly see what Christ has given to us, it moves us to return thanks and give it all back to Him. Like the elders who are honored to sit before God's throne and share in God's government, every glimpse of His glory compels us to fall at His feet and hurl our crowns before His throne in utter abandon.

We have received the costliest gift imaginable. As in the parable of the talents, we must not hide away or bury the treasure we have received. Receiving the glorious life of God moves us to lay aside our glory in gratitude.

Step 3: The Downward Journey

> "...and taking a towel, He girded himself. Then He poured water into the basin and began to wash the disciples' feet and to wipe them with the towel around His waist..." John 13:4-5

> "He emptied himself, taking the form of a servant, and being found in the likeness of men, He humbled Himself and became obedient unto death, even the death of the cross..." Philippians 2:7-8

The Son could have simply retained the Father's love, holding onto the equality with God He had received. That would not have been wrong. The equality was His, by right. However, He did something even better.

Rather than simply bask in the Father's love, the Son poured Himself out, returning everything He received back to the Father.

The Son could have simply remained in Heaven, exchanging glory eternally with the Father. However, in obedience to the Father, He saw a pathway through deepest humility to greater glory.

Philippians shows us a step-by-step description of the Son's downward journey.

Even though He has equality with God, He does not cling to it.

> Instead, He empties Himself (He who has the Fullness)
>> Taking the form of a bond-slave
>> (even though He is the highest ruler)
>>> Then, the uncreated one takes the form of
>>> created man
>>>> Yet again, the great one humbled Himself
>>>> (but how much?)
>>>>> becoming obedient (to what extent?)
>>>>>> to the point of death
>>>>>>> even the lowest form of death:
>>>>>>>> death on a cross.

This is how far Christ has emptied Himself. From greatest glory in the bosom of the Father, possessing all the fullness of God, to deepest humiliation on the cross. He has traversed the entire realm of possible experience—from greatest glory to lowest humility, from highest Heaven to lowest Hell, He has experiential knowledge from pinnacle to pit and now lays claim to every inch.

Knowing this, we can confidently say,

> "neither death, nor life, nor angels, nor principalities, nor things present, nor things to come, nor powers, nor height, nor depth, nor any other created thing will be able to separate us from the love of God which is in Christ Jesus our Lord." Romans 8:38-39

This is how He loved us. This is the pattern we are to follow. This is how our lives will look. And this is how we must love one another. If John 17 unity is our goal, nothing else will get us there.

If our Lord and Master washed our feet, how much more should we wash one another's feet? If the Uncreated One walked this road, how can we as mere creatures scorn it?

If the downward path was good enough for the Master, it is more than good enough for us. Friends, this is the way. It is our highest honor to walk in His footsteps.

Step 4: Exaltation

> "So when He had washed their feet, He took up his mantle and reclined at the table again." John 13:12

> "For this reason, God has highly exalted Him and bestowed on him the name that is above every name so that at the name of Jesus every knee will bow, of those who are in heaven and on earth and under the earth, and that every tongue will confess that Jesus Christ is Lord to the glory of God the Father." Philippians 2:10-11

As the Son completes the downward journey, He commits His Spirit back to the Father's hands. The Son of God is dead. At this exact moment, when the foundations of reality seem to be crumbling and all hope is lost, something unexpected happens.

As He did in the beginning, the Father speaks the Son forth once again: "Let there be light!" Instead of collapse, the Father sends forth His Spirit to inaugurate a new Creation. The Son of God is raised from the dead.

And yet, much was destroyed by the humility of the Son. All lawful claims of Satan and any other spiritual entities to power and dominion over earth and human beings are dissolved. The Son alone, the one in whom all things consist and who upholds all things, has died and risen. The Son alone is the rightful King, not only of Heaven, but also of earth.

The Father, moved by the glorious obedience of His Son, can endure His absence no longer. Jesus ascends to Heaven and is seated at the Father's right hand until all remaining enemies are put under his feet.[6] By His glorious obedience and downward journey, He has won all authority in heaven and on earth. He is Lord of all. He has humbled Himself completely. Now the Father exalts Him to the highest place.

On His coronation day in Heaven, He pours out the Holy Spirit on His brothers.[7] The glory of the heavens is now on earth. The secret of God's inner life is now available to all who believe.

"Have this mind among you"

As we are caught up in the beauty of the divine dance, it is easy to forget the reason Paul has portrayed the humility and glory of the Son in Philippians 2:1-11.

He is showing us the pattern of Jesus's life so that we will do it. We are to love one another like this.

Just as Jesus laid down His life in obedience to the Father, for our benefit, we ought to lay down our lives in obedience to our Father, for the benefit of one another.

And here is the secret of the divine dance. If we follow the downward pattern of the Son in this life, we will also be exalted by the Father and will rule and reign with Him for ever and ever.[8] To the extent that we follow the downward path, to the same extent we will also be exalted by

---

6   Psalm 2 and Acts 2
7   Acts 2
8   See Revelation 5:10

the Father. The lower we go (and I say this with fear), the better.

The price spent on something conveys its value. If the Father valued us with the price of His only begotten Son, how much more should we lavishly spend and pour out our own lives for one another?

Jesus laid aside His robes and washed the disciples' feet. The Son cast aside His heavenly glory in exchange for a life of servanthood, suffering, humiliation, and death.

This is the trajectory our love for one another must take. And not only for one another, but this love must spill over into the world, given freely like sunlight and rain to the righteous and wicked alike.

While our minds may rebel with revulsion and fear at the thought of this downward journey, we must keep in mind the end: to the extent that we follow the Son of Man in humility, we will share with Him in exaltation. "Everyone who exalts himself will be humbled, but all who humble themselves will be exalted."[9] If we will walk like the only-begotten Son, God will treat us like sons and give us a rich portion of His inheritance.

Jesus has laid out the roadmap, showed us the pattern, taught us the dance. But as He says in John 13:17, "If you understand these things, you will be blessed when you do them."

Understanding is not enough. The blessing comes when we put it into action. And for that, we will need something more than a map and a pattern. To love one another as Jesus loved us, we must have divine empowerment. We need experiential knowledge of the love of God.

---

9   Matthew 23:12

3

Experiental Knowledge of Love

As the Wright brothers closed in on a solution to "the flying problem," it became clear the problem of how to fly was actually two distinct problems.

The Wrights had to build a machine that could fly.

They also had to fly a machine they had built.

The second problem was much more dangerous than the first. Building the flying machine was done in the safety of the shop. Plans and blueprints could be studied, modifications made, patterns followed. While the design was difficult, it was not dangerous.

However, stepping into the machine and learning to fly was experiential and involved learning, quite literally, *on the fly*. While Orville and Wilbur had theoretical knowledge of what the controls were supposed to do, they could not know how they worked in practice until the Wright Flyer finally took off.

Speaking in 1901, before their first powered flight, Wilbur compared learning to fly to learning to ride a horse. There were two ways to learn both: "One is to get on [the horse] and learn by actual practice…the other is to sit on a fence and watch the beast…the latter system is safest, but the former…turns out the larger proportion of good riders."[1]

---

1 McCullough, *The Wright Brothers*, 67-68

To learn how to fly, they had to experience flight. And that meant "getting on the horse" and going hundreds of feet off the ground at high speeds years before the invention of a parachute.

Intellectual knowledge was of no use in flight. As Wilbur discovered, "a considerable degree of skill, experience, and sound judgment is required to keep the machine [flying]…a man ought to know that in an emergency his mind and muscles will work by instinct rather than conscious effort. There is no time to think."[2]

It's a wonder that Wilbur never suffered a serious injury despite many close calls and forced landings.[3]

Pattern Alone is Not Enough

In John 13 and Philippians 2, we see how the life of Jesus is the pattern for living in perfect unity with God and with one another. But if we want to live as He lived, pattern alone is not enough.

Although we may see what is required, we lack the inner ability to follow the master in laying down our lives for others. Like middle-aged men watching Olympic gymnasts, we marvel at what is possible while simultaneously understanding, "I will never be able to do that."

Paul spoke of this futility in Romans 7:22-23:

> "For I joyfully concur with the law of God in the inner man, but I see a different law in the members of my body, waging war against the law of my mind…"

While knowing the pattern or having the map is indispensable, it is insufficient. Pattern alone is like building an airplane without ever learning how to fly it.

---

2 *The Wright Brothers*, 92

3 Orville, on the other hand, had a serious crash in 1908 that killed a man and left him in the hospital for seven weeks. The early days of flight claimed many lives.

The Pattern Points to Experiential Knowledge

The only thing that can get us airborne is experiential knowledge of the love of God. If we want to love like Jesus, we need to experience the Father's love just as Jesus experienced it (John 17:26). Truly, we can only love "because He first loved us."

In fact, that is what the pattern itself taught us.

The first step in the John 13 and Philippians 2 roadmap is to know our identity and receive the Father's love. If we are not first undone by His beauty and overwhelmed by His love, we will never have the courage to lay down our lives for His glory.

Thankfully, Jesus has promised us that the same person of the Trinity who communicates the Father's love to Him is now within us. The same person who makes Jesus and the Father one is living in you, longing to answer Jesus's prayer. The experiential knowledge of God's love that Jesus has always known is currently available to every believer by the gift of the Holy Spirit.

The Apostolic Prayers and John 17

Because this is true, it should come as no surprise that when the New Testament authors pray for believers, they continually pray for them to have experiential knowledge of the love of God.

The inspired prayers of Scripture are always looking forward to God's ultimate goals, stating ahead of time what the Father wants to do. The Apostolic Prayers[4] are some of the "other seats in the stadium" where we can look forward into the same glorious future Jesus prays for in John 17.

---

4   Prayers composed by the Apostles.

Philippians 1:9-11: Overflowing Love

> "and this I pray, that your love may abound [overflow, expand] more and more in real [experiential] knowledge and all discernment, so that you may distinguish between things that differ [between good and evil] in order to be sincere and without blame in the day of Christ, having been filled up with the fruit of righteousness that comes through Jesus Christ, to the glory and praise of God."[5]

Paul's greatest prayer for the Philippians is for their love for one another to overflow and abound into *epignosis*.

This Greek word is perhaps best translated "experiential knowledge." We might say "real knowledge" as opposed to book learning or head knowledge. This idea is very similar to the Hebrew word *yada* that speaks of an intimate kind of knowing, the way friends know one another or even more intimately, the "knowing" between a husband and a wife. In other words, Paul is talking about "knowing" how to fly the airplane.

God's love is the source, pouring into the Philippians. They are God's pitchers, pouring love out. In Paul's thinking, love is flowing out from believers like sap flows up a tree. As the sap flows up, it takes on different forms, becoming part of the trunk, a branch, a leaf, or even fruit. Similarly, love flows from us like sap, transforming into experiential knowledge that enables us to walk like Jesus, and discernment between good and evil, which keeps us from sin. Ultimately, this love becomes the fruit of righteous action, something that will endure forever and bring eternal praise to God the Father through Jesus Christ. The source of all this goodness is the overflowing love of God abounding in the hearts of God's new humanity.

---

5   My translation

The imagery of fruit here, along with language about discernment and wisdom harkens back to one of the first trees in the Bible, the Tree of the Knowledge of Good and Evil. God's new humanity is meant to demonstrate the proper way to access knowledge. Real knowledge is not gained by rebellion against God, but through experiential knowledge of His love.

Ephesians 1:15-23: The Fullness Him who Fills All in All

Today's prayers point to tomorrow's reality.

If this is true of our prayers as believers, how much more so for the prayers recorded in Scripture? Biblical prayers predict the future. They are hope-filled and prophetic about what will surely take place. Jesus gets what He prays for. But so does the apostle Paul.

The book of Ephesians contains two of the most powerful prayers recorded in the Bible. Found in Ephesians 1:15-23 and in Ephesians 3:14-21, these are Paul's prophetic prayers for a glorious Church on earth before the Lord's return.

> "For this reason, ever since I heard about your faith in the Lord Jesus and your love for all the saints [God's people on earth], I have not stopped giving thanks for you, making mention of you in my prayers. I keep asking that the God of our Lord Jesus Christ, the Father of glory, *may give you the Spirit of wisdom and revelation in the [experiential] knowledge of Him.*
> I pray that the eyes of your heart may be enlightened in order that you may know the hope of his calling, the riches of his glorious inheritance in the saints [in you and other believers], and his incomparably great power for us who believe." Ephesians 1:15-19a

Paul prays for believers to have "the Spirit of wisdom and revelation" so we can know God. The person and ministry of the Holy Spirit is the focal point of Paul's prayer.[6]

As in Philippians 1:9, the word *epignosis* is used, speaking of experiential knowledge. Paul is not praying for the Holy Spirit to fill us with head knowledge about God or the contents of a systematic theology textbook. He is praying for us to know Father God through the Spirit in the same way we might know a friend, a spouse, or our earthly father. He is asking for relational, experiential knowledge of God.

His prayer for believers to know God is incredibly similar to Jesus's words in John 17:3: "And this is eternal life, *that they might know you*, the only true God, and Jesus Christ who you have sent."

Paul prays for the eyes of our heart to be enlightened to the things of God. This cry is reminiscent of Jesus praying to behold and receive the Father's glory in John 17:1-5, and of Moses crying out "show me your glory" in Exodus 33.

It sounds like David's prayer in Psalm 27:4:

> "One thing have I asked of the LORD, that I will seek: that I may dwell in the house of the LORD all the days of my life, to gaze on the beauty of the LORD and to seek him in his temple."

Over and over, we hear this prayer on the lips of righteous people: "open the eyes of my heart to see your glory."

Paul is not primarily praying for something new to happen. He wants the Holy Spirit to open our eyes to *who we already are in Christ*. He wants us to realize the outrageous hope of our calling, the riches of God's inheritance in us, and His incomparable power that lives in us.

---

6   In speaking about wisdom and revelation, Paul likely has in mind Isaiah 11 and the seven-fold Spirit of God. Revelation gives us experiential knowledge of the things of God. Wisdom allows us to apply that knowledge in our lives.

Chapter 3: Experiential Knowledge of Love

He wants us to realize the miracle. God Himself is dwelling in us!

While Paul wants the Father to give us more of the Spirit, it is so we will become aware of what we already have, that we are "seated in heavenly places with Christ."[7] Paul is praying for the Holy Spirit to open our eyes to what is already true.

His prayer continues:

> "That power [working in you now by the Holy Spirit] is the same as the mighty strength he exerted when he raised Christ from the dead and seated him at his right hand in the heavenly realms, far above all rule and authority, power and dominion, and every name that is invoked, not only in the present age but also in the one to come. And God placed all things under his [Jesus's] feet and appointed him to be head over everything for the church, which is his body, the fullness of him who fills everything in every way." Ephesians 19b-23

Paul reminds us once again of the potency of the gift of the Holy Spirit to human beings. The same Holy Spirit working in us at this very moment is the one who resurrected Jesus from the dead and the same power that brought Him into Heaven, where He sits now at the Father's right hand possessing all authority and dominion. This is the one who was poured out on us, and now is in us.

As the prayer reaches a climax, you might think that phrase "the fullness of Him who fills all in all" is referring to Jesus. However, "the fullness of Him who fills all in all" actually refers to us, to the church.[8]

Think about this: Everything in heaven and earth is under Christ's

---

7 Using his language from Ephesians 2.
8 The New Testament applies the term "church" or "assembly" (Gr. *Ekklesia*) to three different groups. A local church (the church that meets in someone's home), a city-wide or regional church (the church of Ephesus), and the universal church (all believers in Jesus Christ). Here, Paul is clearly speaking about the third group, all believers in Jesus Christ.

feet, and the Father has given Christ to the church as a gift. He is our Head. We are His body. We are His fullness. Together with Christ, we will fill all things in heaven and on earth. What a glorious destiny! What hope! What an outrageous elevation beyond our wildest dreams!

The language of "fullness" is familiar from earlier passages. It is a word that comes out of God's inner life. The Father gave the fullness to the Son. Now, the Son gives His fullness to us. Wherever the word "fullness" is used, look around: the Holy Spirit is there. Once again, the apostle envisions and prays for a future, glorious church that grows into the fullness and maturity that belongs to Christ.

Using the body paradigm, we will be spiritually mature and well fitted to our head as opposed to the ugliness of a large, adult head on a child's body. Using the marriage paradigm, we will be equally yoked in marriage, a mature husband and a mature wife. We will surely be a second Eve suitable and comparable to the second Adam, ready to fill heaven and earth with the glory of her Lord, just as Eve helped Adam fill the earth with people. This is what Paul is praying for in Ephesians 1. He's praying for the Church to become "the fullness of Him who fills all in all."

It's John 17 all over again from another seat in the stadium.

Ephesians 3: 14-21: Knowledge of the Love of God

While it is hard to believe, Ephesians 1:15-23 is only the second-best prayer in the book of Ephesians. Ephesians 3:14-21 is Paul's greatest prayer. It is surpassed only by John 17 in the entire Bible.

> "For this reason, I bow my knees before the Father, from whom the whole family [of believers] in heaven and on earth is named, that according to the riches of his glory, he may grant you to be strengthened with power through his Spirit in your inner man..." Eph. 3:14-16

The Greek word *patria*, translated "family," is often translated as applying to all of humanity. Paul doesn't use this word often, but from the context, it is clear that Paul is praying not for unsaved nations, or the whole human race, but for the family of believers, those who have already received the Holy Spirit. Once again, this is a prayer for the church.

Now, rather than praying for wisdom and revelation on the inside of believers, Paul prays for the power of the Spirit to strengthen them. Why do they need this abundant inner power?

> "So that Christ may dwell in your hearts through faith—that you, being rooted and grounded in love, may have strength to comprehend along with all the saints what is the breadth and length and height and depth, to know the love of Christ that surpasses knowledge, that you may be filled to all the fullness of God." Eph. 3:17-19

Paul's prayer is once again for the Spirit's power to experientially know God's love in all its dimensions. Here, he does not use the Greek word *epignosis* but instead gets the same idea home by saying that knowledge of this love *surpasses knowledge* (*gnosis*). He is communicating the same idea using slightly different words.

The parallels between this prayer and John 17 are everywhere.

The entire family is under the Father's name (John 17:11-12). The riches of the Father's *glory* is the key operating factor in this prayer (John 17:1-5). This glory is released with divine power into the inner part of each believer (John 17:22). The primary revelation of this powerful glory is the love of Christ which surpasses knowledge (John 17:26). Being filled with the love of Christ corporately leads to a future state of fullness (John 17:23). Once again, the Holy Spirit is the key mediator of everything that is happening.

Is there a better description of the "perfect unity" of John 17:23 than the entire church "being filled to all the fullness of God?"

Nearly every key word in Jesus's prayer also appears in Ephesians 3: the Father's name, the glory of God, and divine love. Both prayers emphasize how God's divine nature, His inner life, is now freely shared with human beings. Both prophesy the church's glorious end state.

After essentially praying the biggest prayer He can imagine, Paul declares:

> "Now to Him who is able to do exceedingly abundantly above all that we ask or think, according to the power that works in us, to him be glory in the church and in Christ Jesus throughout all generations, for ever and ever! Amen." Eph. 3:20-21

In other words, "even though I've prayed the biggest prayer I can imagine, it has not scratched the surface of what God is going to do." We have struggled to believe that Jesus gets what He prays for. Here, Paul seems to imply his prayer and even John 17 are merely the tip of the iceberg. God has so much more in store for us, more than we could ever imagine. His goodness is going to keep getting better and better.

Paul continues to emphasize that his impossible prayer will be fulfilled "by the power that works in us." We are gloriously included in God's supernatural activity by the indwelling Spirit, looped into God's inner circle. And the Spirit will not stop until all of us are "filled to all the fullness of God."

There is no way around it. Ephesians 3:14-21 is Paul's John 17 prayer. They're both asking for the same thing, a glorious Church filled with the love of God. Both Jesus and Paul are going to get what they pray for.

The Inner Experience of God's Love

To learn the culture of heaven, the dance of the Father and the Son, to learn to love like God we must first experience God's love. Experiential knowledge of His love is the only thing that can break us out of the world's mind-trap, break us out of the orphanage, and into the Father's house. The experiential love of God through the power, wisdom, and revelation of the Spirit is our only hope to walk out the pattern of Philippians 2 and John 13 that leads to perfect unity. It's the key to seeing the prayers of Philippians 1, Ephesians 1, and Ephesians 3 answered.

The disciples spent three and a half years under Jesus's teaching, receiving training directly from the Son of God. They knew the pattern. And yet, after receiving the best training from the greatest teacher of all time, Jesus marvels at their inability to understand.

And yet, once they receive the gift of the Holy Spirit, they are transformed, making more progress in a day than they had in years. What changed?

The Spirit is the bond of union between the Father and the Son. He is the one who conveys the Father's begetting love to the Son and the Son's obedient love back to the Father. He unites them in perfect love.

How can human beings be one as the Father and Son are one? Only by receiving the love of the Father from the Spirit, just as Jesus received it, and then giving it to one another by the same Spirit.

How can we learn to fly and follow the pattern of life Jesus laid out for us? Only by experiential knowledge of the love of God.

4

John 17, the Nations, and Israel

John 17 unity is not just about individuals. It is also about the nations. So far, we have hardly mentioned this major element. But, if we fail to see Jesus's prayer from this perspective, our vision and expectation will be dangerously flawed.

The High Priestly Prophecy: Make the Nations One

In John 11:49-52, Caiaphas the high priest utters an unknowing prophecy as he calls for the death of Jesus:

> "You know nothing at all, nor do you consider that it is expedient for us that one man should die for the people, and not that the whole nation should perish."

John interprets his counsel to kill the Messiah this way:

> "[Caiaphas] did not say this on his own; but being high priest that year he prophesied that Jesus would die for the nation, and not for that nation [Israel] only but also that He would *gather together in **one*** the children of God who were scattered abroad."

Notice how John expands Caiphas's prophecy beyond his intended meaning of the nation of Israel to include the people of God from all nations. This passage clearly foreshadows Jesus's climactic prayer, "Let them be one as we are one."[1]

John's Gospel has a very intentional structure in two parts. Chapters 1-11 are about Jesus's life and ministry. Chapters 12-21 focus on a much shorter period around His death and resurrection. Caiphas's prophecy comes right at the end of part one. The added context of John 11 makes it abundantly clear that Jesus has people from every nation in mind when He prays a few chapters later.

The fullness of John 17 unity must include people from every nation.

The Great Commission and John 17

Matthew 28:18-20 is perhaps the most famous passage in the New Testament. As Jesus prepares to depart, He issues His final instructions:

> "Go and make disciples of *all nations*, baptizing them in the name of the Father, Son, and Holy Spirit, and teaching them to observe all things that I have commanded you and surely I am with you always, to the very end of the age."

This commissioning comes at the beginning of one age, the age of the New Covenant that would begin on Pentecost a few days later and applies until the end of that age,[2] when the Lord returns. The work

---

[1] John's Gospel is especially important for determining exactly what Jesus is praying for in John 17. The rest of the book is teaching us how to read Jesus's prayer.

[2] Jesus often uses the term "age," most often when speaking about the "end of the age." It speaks of eras or epochs of time. We can consider the first age of human history to be from creation to the creation of Israel and the nations. From Abraham to Christ is a second age, focused on God's activity through His first nation. And from Christ (some would say His birth, others Pentecost, others the destruction of Jerusalem in 70 A.D.) until He returns is the current age. When He returns to rule and reign, that will be "the age to come." However, Paul hints that there are "future ages" awaiting us, so there is much that we do not know about our forever future in Christ.

of the church is not finished until people from *all nations* have been baptized in the faith and trained in Jesus's commandments.

Matthew 24:14 is a parallel passage:

> "The Gospel of the Kingdom will be preached in the whole world as a testimony to all nations [*ethnos*] and then the end will come."

Here, Jesus is even more explicit: our current age will not end, Jesus will not return, until all nations have heard the good news of the Kingdom. One of the major events that must happen before the end of this age is the declaration of the gospel to every people.

In the west, we normally think of nations as "nation-states." We often forget that nation-states are a recent creation. In God's eyes "the nations" include much smaller divisions. The Greek word for nations, "*ethnos*," refers to ethnic groups, not nation states. In other words, Jesus is saying that every culturally distinct group of people, speaking every language, from all over the earth will hear the gospel before He returns.

This reality came home to me on a recent visit to Africa. One of my hosts quite sensibly asked what tribe I belonged to in the United States. I tried to explain how my ancestors had come from across the ocean to live in America, and that most people in the United States did not belong to a tribe. However, it was clear from his facial expressions he had no idea what I was talking about. My normal world made no sense to him at all. He could trace his tribe, their territory, and his tribal language back indefinitely. Everyone that he knew in Uganda belonged to a tribe. This is the normal human experience. My normal as an American is the exception.

When Jesus says the gospel will go to all nations (*ethnos*), He is speaking to people who think like my African friend, not to twenty-first century Americans.

Scripture is crystal clear that our current age will not end until every *ethnic group* has heard the gospel preached to them. After almost 2,000 years, this has still not taken place. In fact, between two to three billion human beings belong to unreached people groups—ethnic nations that have never heard the gospel.[3]

John 17 cannot be fulfilled without them.

Revelation 7: The Nations in John 17 Unity

In Revelation 7, the prophet sees an astoundingly massive crowd of worshippers,

> "...from every nation, tribe, people, and language standing before the throne and before the Lamb, clothed with white robes, with palm branches in their hands, and crying out with a loud voice, 'Salvation belongs to our God who sits on the throne, and to the Lamb!'" Revelation 7:9-10

One of the twenty-four elders who sits near the throne in the presence of God provides the interpretation of the vision to John:

> "These are the ones who came out of the great tribulation and washed their robes and made them white in the blood of the Lamb. Therefore, they are before the throne of God and serve Him day and night in His temple. And He who sits on the throne will dwell among them." Rev. 7:14-15

In this passage, we see an uncountable group of worshippers from every nation on earth who have emerged from the greatest period of trial and tribulation in human history. Despite the great suffering and the immense size and diversity of the group, they are all holy and pure,

---

3   www.joshuaproject.net is a great resource to become familiar with the idea of Unreached People Groups, ethnic nations that have not yet received the gospel.

dressed symbolically in white. These worshippers minister directly to God's throne and experience Him dwelling in their very midst.

If Matthew 24 and Matthew 28 are the marching orders to bring in every nation, Revelation 7 is a prophetic picture of the end state. Here, we see conclusive proof, if we needed it, that this group contains not only "nations," but smaller divisions as well: "…every tribe…and language."

The similarities between Revelation 7 and John 17 are everywhere. The multitude is assembled from every nation and tribe. They are united in glory-filled worship. They are holy, pure, and spotless, "sanctified in the truth." Once again, unity is corporate holiness. The two cannot be separated.

Revelation 7:9-17 is yet another perspective describing what Jesus prayed for in John 17. We ought to add to our understanding from this passage that the incredible holiness and unity that Jesus prays for will emerge in the context of the greatest period of testing and trouble the earth has ever seen. It is remarkable to realize that in John 16, the immediate context of Jesus's prayer, is about enduring trial and tribulation. John 18 and 19 on the other side are about His moment of greatest trial.

Putting these different perspectives together, a clear vision begins to emerge: the Father is bringing into complete unity a family from every culture, tribe, nation, and language through the blood of His Son, and the powerful working of the Holy Spirit. This group will emerge in perfect unity once all the nations are included and will gain purity and holiness during a time of unprecedented testing and tribulation.

Clearly, God is passionately committed to the nations. Before this age can end, people from every tribe and language will respond to the gospel and be made "perfectly one." Not one ethnic nation can be left out.

However, to really understand why every nation is so important to God, we need to go back to the beginning of the story. We need to see why God created the nations.

The Nations in Scripture

For some reason, Noah's flood is thought of as a children's story. It has animals, rainbows, a big boat, and a kindly, bearded old man. I can see new parents covering their first child's room with wallpaper of Noah's Ark and the animals, walking two-by-two.

In reality, Noah's flood is the most severe judgement on humanity in human history. All but eight people were killed—wiped out by God's righteous wrath.

God is a more patient person than we can imagine. However, at a certain point sin and evil become so great that in His justice He must respond. This happens in the pre-flood world—the evil of humanity becomes so intense, God must wipe everything out. He spares only eight people.

On the other side of the flood, God makes a new covenant with humanity never again to destroy every living creature.

> "Never again will I curse the ground because of humans, even though every inclination of the human heart is evil from childhood. And never again will I destroy all living creatures, as I have done. As long as the earth endures, seedtime and harvest, cold and heat, summer and winter, day and night, will never cease." Genesis 8:20-22

As we can see, God makes this promise to humanity while fully aware that "every inclination of the human heart is evil from childhood."

This seems like good news. God promises not to use this extreme measure of judgement on mankind. He wants to be kind to humanity.

On the other hand, our malevolent, evil, and ignorant ways threaten to destroy the earth. How can He reconcile His kindness towards us with the need for justice? The pre-flood world quickly devolved into utter evil, violence, and demonic chaos leading to God's judgement. With this option off the table, how will God keep the earth from devolving into a horrific hellscape?

To avoid unbearable wickedness, God will introduce mitigation measures designed to restrain and contain human evil.

The Nations: God's Evil Mitigation Plan

First, even before the flood in Genesis 6:3, God reduces the lifespan of human beings from around 900 years to 120 years. A decreasing lifespan limits the impact of an evil person. Can you imagine what Mao, Stalin, and Hitler would have done if they could have expected to live hundreds of years?

By the time Moses wrote Psalm 90 around 1400 B.C., the average lifespan had been further reduced to its current norm, seventy to eighty years. The futility of death is one way God limits human evil.

However, God has an even more strategic plan to frustrate human evil: He divides humanity into seventy different groups with different languages, cultures, and customs (Genesis 10).[4] God creates the nations as His ultimate evil-mitigation plan.

Genesis 11 gives us more detail on how the nations were created, and why God had to divide humanity to prevent evil from metastasizing. The citizens of Babel, which sounds like "confusion" in Hebrew, were intent on resisting God's mandate to fill the earth. Instead, they chose to build a city and a tower for their own fame and glory. God recognized

---

4   The genealogy of the nations in Genesis 10 lists seventy nations. For this reason, the numbers seven, seventy, and their derivatives are highly symbolic elsewhere in Scripture of all the nations.

that because of their unity, they would accomplish all their evil desires. The growth of wickedness would quickly get out of control because they were one. So that He could have mercy on them, He confused their evil unity by creating different languages and nations.

The confusion of languages caused them to disperse throughout the earth. The propagation of evil through one united human civilization would have destroyed the earth in just a few generations.

The nations are God's plan to keep the earth from being judged prematurely. Our different cultures and languages are a necessary friction that prevents the entire planet from sliding into chaos. One nation may become extremely evil—think Nazi Germany or Japan in the 1930s and '40s—but the other nations, while also corrupt to some degree, keep extremes of evil in check. National and linguistic boundaries are firewalls that keep evil from breaking out and filling the entire earth.

Finally, and most importantly, out of these scattered nations, the Creator chooses one nation for Himself, promising to bless all the nations of the earth through one man, Abram.

And so we see that while God creates the nations to limit human evil (and postpone His just judgment), His heart in the midst of it all is to bless every nation on earth and bring them back together *as one* under His chosen Messiah.

God Chooses a Nation

Immediately after God divides the nations in Genesis 11, we begin to see God's reunification plan in action in Genesis 12:1-3.

> "Now the LORD said to Abram: Get out of your country, from your family and from your father's house to a land that I will show you. I will make you a great nation; I

will bless you and make your name great and you shall be a blessing. I will bless those who bless you and I will curse him who curses you; and *in you all the families of the earth shall be blessed.*"

God's plan to reunite all the families of the earth post-Babel begins with the claiming of one family and one nation as His own, the line of Abram and the nation of Israel. Incredibly, for the next 2,000 years, His plan and purpose will focus on this one small nation.

God gives the other nations of the world over to their own evil ways, to worship idols, demons, and false gods. In essence, the Creator says to the dark spiritual powers: "For now, you can have the rest of the nations. I'll just take this one family, barely even a nation, as my own."[5]

And yet, His promise remains: to bless all nations through one nation.

Starting with Abram, God pours Himself into Israel, establishing His covenant with the patriarchs, bringing deliverance from slavery, revealing His Law through Moses, giving them the promised land under Joshua, and uniting them as a kingdom under David and Solomon. While Israel often suffered judgement for their unfaithfulness, God never turned away from the apple of His eye. Even when He punished them and scattered them among the nations, He used them as a prophetic people. Scattered Israel established synagogues and schools, creating outposts throughout the ancient world where the one true God was worshipped and known. Many people from the nations began to worship the God of Israel.

However, the culmination of God's work in Israel came when the Son of God Himself, Jesus Christ, took on flesh. The Messiah, the desire of all nations, came forth from the first nation that God chose

---

5   See Deut. 32:8-9 and Acts 17:26-31

for Himself. God's plan to bless all the nations through Abraham was coming to a culmination—the promised one had come!

Natural Israel in the New Covenant

However, something incredibly strange and unexpected happened when the Israeli Messiah, the King of the Jews, appeared on the scene. Most of the nation God had prepared 2,000 years for this very moment, including their entire ruling class, rejected their Messiah. And instead, the pagan nations surrounding Israel received and accepted the Jewish King as their own. Within 300 years of the birth of the church, even the mighty Roman Empire would bow the knee to King Jesus while the vast majority of Israel continued in unbelief.

Imagine how strange it would be if Muhammed were acknowledged as a prophet by every nation, except the Arabs. Or if Hinduism were practiced around the world but despised in India. Imagine if Bach were celebrated as a great musician in Japan, China, and Nigeria, but reviled in Austria and Germany. Or if DaVinci was considered a genius around the globe, but a hack and a fraud by Italians.

And yet, this is exactly what has happened with Jesus. Only a very small number of ethnic Jews and Israelis worship the Jewish Messiah who is believed on by more than a third of the peoples of the earth from all over the globe. Still to this day, the world's most famous Jew is an outcast among His own people. We would be excused for thinking that God was finished with His first nation, the nation of Israel. After all, even at the beginning of that nation, we saw the goal—to bless and reunite all the nations of the earth. It might seem as though Israel has already served its purpose.

Romans 9-11

In Romans chapters 9-11, the Apostle Paul gives us a deeper vision into what has happened.

While the majority of natural Israel has rejected their Messiah, God has preserved a remnant of believers from His first nation. The mystery that was hidden from past generations, the upside-down plan of God, is for the gospel to go to all the nations, and then to return to Israel, the first nation, last of all—so that the first nation will be the last nation to say "yes" to God's reunification plan of all nations under His chosen ruler.[6]

Because the gospel was readily adopted by many other nations, and rejected by most Jews, Paul knew there would be a tendency to think that God was finished with his first nation. After all, in one sense, in the New Covenant it no longer matters what our nation of origin is—we are all equal in Christ.[7]

However, the truth of the matter is more complicated and more incredible. The Father's plan is to somehow open the eyes of the unbelieving Jewish people, His first nation, to their own national Messiah at a moment very close to the return of the Lord Jesus. As Romans 11:15 says, "if their [natural Israel's] being cast away is the reconciling of the world [the nations], what will their acceptance be but life from the dead [the resurrection]?"

The Father is not finished with His first nation. He is using Gentile nations to stir Israel to jealousy. Someday soon, the blinders will fall from their eyes and "they will look upon the one whom they have pierced and mourn as for an only son and grieve for Him as one grieves for a firstborn."[8]

Israel and the Nations

In the final week before His crucifixion, Jesus wept over Jerusalem, seeing the destruction that was coming to the beloved city. He prophesied the

---

6   Romans 11:1-15
7   Gal. 3:28
8   Zech. 12:10

destruction of the city and the temple,⁹ a righteous judgment for the sins of that generation and the sins of Israel for generations.¹⁰ He told the rulers of the city that they would not see Him again until they declared, "Blessed is He who comes in the name of the LORD."¹¹

In A.D. 70, Jerusalem was destroyed by the Romans, and the Jewish people scattered.

Somehow, in spite of not having a homeland for almost 1900 years, they retained a distinct culture, worship, and language. In 1948, after nearly being wiped out by a demonic ruler, this wandering nation returned to its historic homeland. In 1967, Jerusalem came back into Israeli control.

The nation of Israel is somehow back on the national scene after a 1900-year absence. This is truly remarkable. No other nation has lost its homeland for almost two millennia and still maintained a national identity. And yet, even more remarkable is that spiritually, the Israel of today is nearly identical to what Paul describes in the first century. There is a small remnant of Jews who have believed in their Messiah,¹² and yet the vast majority reject the Jewish Messiah who is worshipped by one-third of the human race.

We find ourselves in a very similar situation to the first century, except with this one change: the journey of the gospel to every tribe, language, and nation is nearly complete. Just as Jesus predicted, the gospel has gone out from Jerusalem, Judea, and Samaria into the utter ends of the earth. Now, from the ends of the earth, the gospel is making its way back to Jerusalem.

---

9   Matthew 23-24
10 Luke 11:49-51
11 Matt. 23:39
12 See Romans 11:5-6

John 17, Israel, and the Nations

History is moving towards a John 17 climax, a unity in the Spirit among followers of Jesus that has never been seen. As we can now clearly see, the full answer to Jesus's prayer in John 17 must include people from every tribe, nation, language, and people. It must also include believers from God's first nation, the nation of Israel and the Jewish diaspora.

In fact, a closer reading of Revelation 7, focusing on verses 4-8, presents this exact picture. Here we see a remnant of Israel included alongside every nation in the assembly of the redeemed. Not only is there a great multitude present from every tribe and language but there are also 144,000 Israelis, 12,000 from every tribe present along with the uncountable multitude from the nations. This same group is later found in Revelation 14, standing with the Messiah on Mt. Zion in Jerusalem, singing a new song as first-fruits of the age to come.

Imagining the End of the Age

While I do not understand how this will play out in detail, I am not blind to the pattern: A remnant of Israel and a multitude from every nation are both essential to God's end of the age plan.

We can be assured that as we move towards the Lord's return, a dynamic, glorious, and visible oneness will characterize followers of Jesus from every tribe, nation, and language, including the remnant of Jews and Israelis who know their Messiah. As the gospel increases to include more and more nations, we should anticipate this grace for John 17 unity to increase.

I am not entirely certain of the order of these related events. John 17:23 declares that the evidential power of "perfect oneness" will cause the entire world to acknowledge that Jesus was sent by the Father. One possibility is that the oneness of God's people will be the capstone that completes the Great Commission. Or perhaps it is the other way around and the completion of the Great Commission, the inclusion of people from every tribe and language in the body of Christ, will trigger this glorious unity.

Either way, it is abundantly evident that John 17 unity and the fulfillment of the Great Commission are future realities that function hand in glove. They cannot be separated.

In a similar way, the salvation of the nations and of God's first nation are inextricably linked together.

Could it be that the fulfillment of John 17 is the witness that finally stirs blind and unbelieving Israel to jealousy for their own Messiah? Or is it the other way around, will the turning of Israel to their Messiah be the missing piece that makes John 17 unity possible?

The exact sequence of how these events unfold remains shrouded in mystery. But this much is clear from Genesis to Revelation: A full answer to Jesus's prayer in John 17 requires people every tribe, nation, people, and language. And it requires people from God's first nation, Israel.

God subjected the nations to futility, not willingly, but in hope.[13] Now, He is bringing them all together again, by the power of His Spirit, in His beloved Son.

We are approaching the moment when all things will be made one in the Messiah, things in heaven, and earth.[14]

---

13 Romans 8:20
14 Ephesians 1:10

5

Pioneers of Spirit and Sky

On January 1, 1901, as the twentieth century dawned, Pope Leo XIII entered St. Peter's Basilica in Rome, singing the song *Veni Creator Spiritus*, "Come, Holy Spirit." He entered the ornate church for a special purpose: to dedicate the new century to the Holy Spirit.

Sister Elena Guerra, a prophetic nun known for her piety and good works, had written him repeatedly, pleading with him for a renewed devotion to the Holy Spirit in the church and specifically to dedicate the new century to the Holy Spirit. The Pope responded, adding his apostolic authority to her prophetic invitation.

A few hours later on the same day, at the tiny Bethel Bible school in Topeka, Kansas, Agnes Ogman experienced the baptism of the Holy Spirit accompanied by speaking in tongues. It was the first modern, documented case of speaking in tongues.

Somehow, the prayer of a Pope had landed in Kansas.[1]

Today, more than 120 years later, hundreds of millions of believers use the gift of tongues as a daily part of their prayer lives. Unlike 1901,[2] most Christians globally believe the gifts of the Spirit like prophecy and

---

1 See *The Charismatic Century*, pg. 1 by Jack Hayford
2 For more research on changes in Christianity over the past 120 years, see the Lausanne Movements "State of the Great Comission Report" https://lausanne.org/report.

healing are for today. Charismatic and Pentecostal movements, totaling over 600 million people, are the most dynamic, fastest-growing part of the church.[3] Even people who don't believe in speaking in tongues, healing, or prophecy have been impacted by the music and culture of those who are "filled with the Spirit." It is hard to imagine a time before this was normal.[4]

The twentieth century was indeed, as Jack Hayford said, "The Charismatic Century." As a charismatic myself, it's hard to imagine life without the gifts of the Spirit—why would we ever want to go back? I've given and received accurate prophetic words, witnessed healings, miracles, baptisms of the Spirit, and many of the other gifts, manifestations, and workings of the Holy Spirit. This is simply normal, New Testament Christianity.

Historic Precedents

For a believer living in the year 1900, the everyday church life of believers today where the gifts of the Spirit are normal would seem bizarre and difficult to imagine, like something they had only read about in the Bible.

Today, we are in a similar situation as it relates to John 17. We read Jesus's prayer and stretch out our faith to say, "Jesus gets what He prays for," but our vision of this future promise is cloudy, and the path forward uncertain. We have never seen John 17 unity.

---

3   The Center for the Global Study of Christianity at Gordon-Conwell has extensive research on the global church and the embrace of the gifts of the Spirit, including https://www.gordonconwell.edu/wp-content/uploads/sites/13/2024/01/Status-of-Global-Christianity-2024.pdf. To list just one of many articles that reference their research, https://www.christianitytoday.com/2020/05/holy-spirit-empowered-christian-global-pentecostal-study/.

4   Anecdotally, when I travel outside the western world I have yet to meet a believer who does not believe that the gifts of the Spirit are for today.

Chapter 5: Pioneers of Spirit and Sky

One way to fuel our faith and imagine this seismic shift prophesied by Scripture is by looking at historic precedents where the impossible became the new normal.

We'll explore two breakthroughs that took place at the turn of the twentieth century. One is natural, the other spiritual: the Wright brothers and the invention of the first airplane, and William Seymour and the birth of modern Pentecostalism.

The Wright Brothers at Kitty Hawk

As the humble Bethel Bible School was pioneering speaking in tongues and rediscovering the baptism of the Spirit, the Wright brothers were engaged in another impossible experiment: the construction of a heavier-than-air flying machine.

Thousands of years of human history testified with a common voice: flight was impossible. Brilliant minds like Leonardo DaVinci had explored the idea to no avail. Heavier-than-air flight was a fools' errand, an irrational and impractical waste of time.

And yet, Orville and Wilbur looked to the heavens. Birds were heavier than air, and yet they could fly. If a bird could fly, so could a man. Brilliantly, they broke down the complexity of the bird's moving wing propulsion into stationary wings with a fixed power system. They broke down flight mechanics into three independent planes of motion, with control surfaces for each plane. They built the first wind tunnel to try out scale models of their gliders.

Other new inventions would make their dream possible. The advent of small, gasoline-powered internal combustion engines provided them with a viable power source. A steam boiler could power a ship but was far too large for an airplane where every ounce of weight mattered.

On December 17, 1903, in the obscurity of coastal North Carolina,

Orville Wright made the first powered flight, traversing a mere 120 feet. No crowds were there to witness it. However, the breakthrough of that day, the culmination of years of failure and experimentation, would change the world forever.[5]

William Seymour and the Azusa Street Revival

In the first decade of the twentieth century, powerful moves of God popped up independently around the globe. There was the first modern, documented case of speaking in tongues on January 1, 1901. Then, in short order came the Welsh Revival (1904), Pyongyang Revival in Korea (1907), and Azusa Street Revival in Los Angeles (1906). While these events are well-known, it is important to note that there were also independent moves of God in Pakistan, India, China, and Africa. In hindsight, it is clear: a global outpouring of the Holy Spirit was underway in the first decade of the century. God was moving in a way that had not been seen since the first-century church, and on a global scale.

The Azusa Street outpouring in 1906 was especially influential. Over 600 million charismatic and Pentecostal believers today all trace their lineage through Azusa Street, and the movement has seasoned the rest of the church as well—even those who still reject it.

A One-Eyed Black Man

William Seymour was a black man, a son of former slaves, and blind in one eye.[6] He was a student of Charles Fox Parham, the founder

---

5 *The Wright Brothers*, 105

6 A variety of resources were drawn from in writing this sketch of Seymour and Azusa Street, including *The Charismatic Century* by Jack Hayford (esp. Ch. 4) *Streams of Living Water* by Richard Foster, *True Stories of the Miracles of Azusa Street* by Tom Welchel. Wikipedia and other online resources were consulted as well.

of Bethel Bible school in Topeka, Kansas. In spite of the remarkable experience of January 1, 1901, Bethel had closed just four months later. Parham was soon teaching in Houston, Texas, where Seymour listened to his teachings on the baptism of the Spirit while sitting outside the room. The practice of racial segregation in the southern city kept Seymour out of the main sessions. Despite this humiliating treatment, Seymour ate up the teaching on the baptism of the Spirit, the gifts, and speaking in tongues.

The dominant theology of the time claimed the supernatural gifts of the Holy Spirit, like prophecy, healing, and tongues, had ceased with the apostles after the first century.

Parham, Seymour, and others were the fringe of the fringe, a group of passionate believers who were convinced that God hadn't changed, and He wanted to pour out the gifts afresh on His church. Refusing to believe what everyone thought or the testimony of their own personal experiences over the promises of the word of God, they were chasing a breakthrough.

In February of 1906, William Seymour received a call to Los Angeles. After his first sermon there, focused on the baptism of the Holy Spirit, Seymour was unceremoniously booted from his new congregation. The doors were literally padlocked to keep him out.

Seymour was a man of sorrows.

Now out on the street and without a job in a strange city, he found refuge with a small group of believers and began a prayer group. This group decided to focus on receiving the baptism of the Spirit with the evidence of speaking in tongues. On April 6, 1906, Seymour and his group began ten days of fasting and prayer, modeled on the ten-day prayer meeting of the early church in Acts 1. They were seeking a new Pentecost.

On April 9, after just three days of prayer, the outpouring began.

Many in the small prayer group were powerfully encountered by the Holy Spirit and began speaking in other languages. Incredibly, one of the women who didn't play the piano began playing flawlessly while singing in multiple known languages, including Hebrew.

Despite this breakthrough, Seymour himself remained barren. Then, on April 12, Seymour himself experienced the baptism and spoke in tongues. At this point, the little house on Bonnie Brae Street in Los Angeles was overflowing. The meeting shifted to an old horse stable not far away on Azusa Street.

The new outpouring was characterized in the press as insane religious fanaticism. And yet, over the next three and a half years, people from around the world came through the Azusa Street Mission. It wasn't just speaking in tongues, either. Powerful healings were happening regularly. Accurate prophetic gifts were in operation. Demons were cast out. Some nights, they even witnessed a visible cloud of God's presence in the congregation, the Shekinah glory.

Hundreds of millions of modern believers trace their spiritual heritage not only through a barn in Bethlehem, but also through a stable in Los Angeles. Because of this breakthrough, the gifts of the Spirit, once thought to be relegated to apostolic times, are in active and regular operation throughout much of the global church.

A New Shift in the Church Age

The Wrights poured over every book they could find related to flight. However, the existing knowledge was not enough. They were on the technological frontier and much of what had been written was false or mistaken.[7] They turned to trial and error, experimentation, failure,

---

7 *The Wright Brothers*, 63, 69

and reiteration. Most of all, they trusted what they learned through experience more than anything they read or heard from others.

Seymour and the Pentecostal Pioneers were on a path of rediscovery. Something that had been normal for the early church, the gifts of the Spirit, was somehow lost through the centuries. Like the Wrights, Seymour had to have faith and persevere through many painful experiences and prolonged fruitlessness to achieve a breakthrough.

All of us have grown up in a world where the breakthroughs achieved by the Wrights and Seymour have matured and become an accepted part of daily life. Flying is still amazing, but we see airplanes flying almost every day. We were born into the world they created. Speaking in tongues is a remarkable gift of the Spirit. It is also something I hear in almost every prayer meeting I attend.

It can be hard to imagine how it must have felt to be part of these moments of historic breakthrough. But, we need to put ourselves in their shoes because in terms of John 17 unity, we are living in the days before flight.

What if we are the new Pioneers, the ones chasing the fullness of God's promises? Similar to Pentecostal Pioneers, our best model for John 17 unity is found in the book of Acts.

What if we keep running experiments on unity until we manage to get the plane in the air? And then keep working until we have a plane that can fly every day? Could it be that an entirely new world is waiting to open itself to us as Jesus's prayer is finally answered?

As potential pioneers of this unity revolution, we need to learn from the triumphs and mistakes of Seymour and the Wright brothers.

Hunger and Perseverance in Hiddenness Leads to Breakthrough

Orville and Wilbur Wright were both bachelors. Wilbur quipped that he "did not have time for both a wife and an airplane," speaking to the single-minded obsession the brothers directed toward "the flying problem." From 1899-1903 the brothers labored in obscurity, investing all they had in their time-consuming hobby. Few people knew of their work and fewer still believed it would succeed. Only five people witnessed the first flight.

Pioneering is hidden work. It's in the secret place that new life is conceived.

However, even after they had gone public with their flying machine, people still did not believe it. As late as 1906, other prominent aviation pioneers were calling them frauds. Local newspapermen in the Wrights' home of Dayton, Ohio, missed out on the story of a lifetime because they thought it was a hoax. The Wright brothers didn't become famous until 1908, when Wilbur demonstrated their airplane in France. Truly, a prophet has no honor in his hometown.

When the Azusa Street Revival broke out, William Seymour was an obscure holiness preacher. For years, his hunger for more of God had led him from place to place. He was always wandering, full of faith there was more of God for him, and yet he never experienced a meaningful breakthrough. Seymour was often treated poorly even by his teachers and experienced racial discrimination regularly. The church he led in 1906 was tiny, with a core group of ten adults and five children. The Bonnie Brae house where the outpouring began looks like every other home in the neighborhood. There was nothing attractive about it. The Azusa Street meetings took place in an old horse stable.

Once again, the breakthrough came in the secret place, to an obscure and unlikely man who was hungry for God and willing to persevere in obscurity until he achieved the breakthrough he had seen by faith.

Pioneers Have Limited Vision

While we celebrate pioneers for seeing what others cannot, they also make serious errors.

Chapter 5: Pioneers of Spirit and Sky

Because they are breaking into unknown territory, some of their ideas turn out to be utterly wrong or useless. Pioneers must be contrarian to persevere against the prevailing wisdom of their day. This same tendency can lead them to reject what they should preserve or have other fringe opinions that turn out to be wrong.

As we imagine a future breakthrough for John 17 unity in the body of Christ, it is worth recognizing this: We are almost certainly wrong about particulars of what this will look like in ways we cannot yet imagine.

While the Wright brothers made the initial breakthrough in flight, some of their ideas about flying were soon discarded.

For instance, the Wrights used a steering technique called "wing warping," bending the entire wing like a bird in flight to roll the plane to the left or right. Almost no future plane designs would use wing warping. Ailerons, smaller, movable parts of wings, are the steering mechanism used on all modern planes.

The Wrights also opposed runways and the use of wheels on airplanes. Instead, they used rails and a kind of catapult to launch the Wright Flyer into the sky. Why would you build a road for something that flies? Or put wheels on a vehicle meant to soar in the sky? To their minds, roads (runways) and wheels for airplanes seemed as odd as wheels on a boat.

The Pentecostal Pioneers also had striking misses.

For instance, they rightly saw the connection between the gift of the Holy Spirit and missions. They concluded from this connection that the gift of tongues was primarily a missionary gift that would make language study for missions obsolete. Some early Pentecostals sailed to foreign nations as missionaries in the mistaken belief that the Holy Spirit would empower them to speak the native language.[8] When

---
8   *The Charismatic Century*, 99-101

they arrived, they started speaking to natives by the Spirit. This led to some embarrassing cross-cultural experiences.

There were other mistaken beliefs related to the baptism, including an expectation that it would prevent people who received it from sinning or that the baptism of the Spirit was a sign that believers were part of the 144,000 in Revelation 7 and that the Lord's return was imminent. While there was often an increase in ability to obey the Lord, the baptism of the Spirit did not transform believers into people who could not sin, nor did 1906 usher in the return of the Lord.

Other mistakes were more serious. Early Pentecostals like Frank Bartleman,[9] the intercessor and chronicler of Azusa Street, rightly believed they had rediscovered a lost element of the apostolic faith. However, this new revelation led him and others to reject aspects of the apostolic faith that had been preserved faithfully by the Church. Tragically, Bartleman and many other early Pentecostals rejected orthodox Trinitarian theology to embrace a "Jesus only" heresy.

Pioneering is Heart-Breaking Work

After changing the world through their invention, the Wrights faced new difficulties. In 1908, Orville was seriously injured in a plane crash that killed his passenger. The early days of flight were dangerous, and they took their lives in their hands on every flight.

The Wrights also became embroiled in legal disputes over their patent claims on the airplane that dragged on for many years, eventually turning public opinion against the brothers. Their lawsuits to maintain patent rights on every airplane made in the States slowed American aircraft innovation, causing Europe to far outpace the Americans in the first two decades of flight. The lawsuits were a drain on their finances and creativity. Ultimately, it kept them from scaling up aircraft

---

9   *The Charismatic Century*, 120-125

production, even though they were first in the business. Other flight pioneers like Glenn Curtiss soon took the baton, vastly improving their designs and pioneering large-scale aircraft production.

Some have speculated that the emotional toll of the patent disputes contributed to the early death of Wilbur from typhoid fever at age 45.

The early Pentecostal movement experienced numerous power-encounters as thousands were impacted by the baptism of the Spirit. However, along with these power encounters came power struggles, leading to painful splits along racial, personal, and theological lines.

Charles Fox Parham, who taught Seymour in Houston, later denounced him because of the racial integration of the Azusa Street meetings. Tragically, this division and others would lead to a segregated Pentecostalism in America. It was said early on that "the color line was erased by the blood." This breakthrough, a supernatural love across racial lines, was lost.

In 1908, Seymour's secretary and editor of the *Apostolic Faith* newsletter, Clara Lum, split with Seymour and ran off with the mailing list. While the revival continued until 1909, it never recovered from this blow, and Seymour's influence began to wane.

Finally, in 1911, Seymour and his dear friend Willam Durham had a theological falling out.[10] Seymour's wife, Jennie, padlocked Durham out of the Azusa Street Mission, just as Seymour was padlocked out when he first came to Los Angeles. Durham went after Seymour publicly, causing a split in the Los Angeles Pentecostal community. By 1914, Seymour's congregation was once again a small, black church, much as it had been when he arrived in Los Angeles. God's chosen vessel to spark a global movement faded back into obscurity. Like John the Baptist, his personal ministry decreased even as the movement he heralded continued to grow around the world.

---

10   *The Charismatic Century*, 118

Seymour passed away in 1922, still a relatively young man, of a double heart attack. It is said that William Seymour died of a broken heart.

Conclusions

Both Wilbur Wright and William Seymour were heralds of a new era who died prematurely before their work came to greater fullness.

As the story of their lives makes clear, history has major moments of change, whether spiritually or naturally, where pioneers make what was once impossible, possible. Ultimately, what was once impossible becomes the new normal for future generations.

We have focused on powered flight and the modern Pentecostal movement, but hundreds of other biblical and historical examples could have been chosen: Jesus's first coming, the Davidic kingdom, the calling of Abraham, the discovery of the New World, the Protestant Reformation, or the making of the atom bomb.

These breakthroughs are cultivated in obscurity and hiddenness. They are birthed into the world through men and women of hunger, faith, and perseverance.

Once these breakthroughs become public, the future they bring often looks far different than the pioneers themselves expected. Those who see the breakthrough coming are often wrong about its implications in ways that are unpredictable. Pioneers often make serious and costly errors.

There are massive dangers on either side of the breakthrough, and even if you see the impossible happen, you may still die in obscurity of a broken heart.

Are we ready to follow downward path of Jesus, Seymour, and even the Wright brothers in our quest to see an answer to Jesus's prayer?

While we are right to move forward with fear and trembling, these examples fill us with hope. While it may seem difficult to imagine a global Church walking in John 17 unity, we have seen the world change dramatically before. The impossible dreams of these pioneers of Spirit and sky have become our new normal.

In terms of John 17, we are living in the days before flight.

Where are the new pioneers who will make the impossible possible, and pull Jesus's dying wish into the present?

6

Signs of Coming Glory

A fundamental transformation is on the horizon, one the world has never seen before: a unity revolution that will turn the world upside down. Like the Wright brothers' first flight, the breakthrough is happening in secret. Small groups of people everywhere are beginning to experience a fresh measure of John 17 unity.

While no one knows for sure, it is possible that we are living in the generation that will see Jesus's prayer answered in fullness. I believe there are at least seven biblical signs that we are approaching the ultimate answer to Jesus's prayer.

Sign 1: The Spread of the Gospel to the Nations

John 17 unity requires people from every tribe, language, people, and nation.

Unity propels mission—when we are one, the world sees who Jesus is. But mission also propels unity—we can't have John 17 in fullness without the all the nations.

For the first time in history, the fulfillment of the Great Commission may be in sight.

In the year 1900, over 80% of the world's Christian population lived in North America and Europe.¹ Less than 8% lived in Africa or Asia. Entire continents were almost untouched by the gospel of Christ. Today, those numbers have flipped, with over 65% of believers now living in Africa, Asia, and Latin America. Africa is on pace to have the most believers of any continent by 2050.

These numbers are based on official government statistics. However, in many places, like China, India, Indonesia, and the Muslim world, believers do not want to be counted for fear of persecution. At the same time, their governments do not want to count them for fear of losing face. On a regular basis, we hear encouraging reports from church networks in Asia and the Middle East. A massive harvest is taking place in our day, a harvest that will never appear in a government census.

Organizations focused on Bible translation are partnering like never before. There is expectation that by 2030, the Bible will be translated into every known language.² That is a historic fulfillment of what Jesus promised. While there are still tribes and peoples that are unreached, the Church is nearer than ever before to a point where members of "every tribe, language, people, and nation" will all worship the Lamb. It seems the table is being set for guests from every nation to be one, just as the Father and Son are one.

In addition to the spread of the gospel to new nations, since 1967 we have seen the re-emergence of distinctly Jewish expression of the faith through the Messianic movement. A small but strong remnant of God's first nation is living in the promised land and worshipping their

---

1 For these statistics and more information on changes in Christianity over the past 120 years, see the Lausanne Movement's "State of the Great Commission Report" https://lausanne.org/report

2 See, for example: https://seedcompany.com/stories/the-ripple-effect-makes-waves-in-asia/. Personal conversations with those involved in Bible translation have emphasized the acceleration that is taking place. 2030 seems like a reasonable goal to complete the translation of the Bible into every language. This is almost exactly 2,000 years after the giving of the Great Commission.

promised Messiah, while also building bridges and friendships with the Church from the nations.

For the first time since the first century, there is a Jewish Church based in Jerusalem.

Sign 2: Technology and Global Connectivity

Jesus's prayer prophesies not only a supernatural intimacy among believers by the Spirit, but also that this union would be experienced by a multi-national communion of saints. According to Scripture, this group must include every single tribe, language, and nation. None can be left out. For the first time in history, the internet has made possible instantaneous and inexpensive communication around the world. During the Covid-19 pandemic of 2020, it was easier to talk with someone in Thailand than to have my neighbor over for dinner.

On a weekly basis, I pray with believers from all six inhabited continents. The ubiquity of the English language makes communication across cultures easier than ever. In fact, we are seeing a common global culture emerge, not unlike what happened in ancient Babel.

Could it be that the divine purpose of the internet and modern travel is to connect and display His people in "perfect unity?"

Sign 3: Increasing Wickedness and Persecution (Two Global Unity Movements)

The flip side of global interconnectedness is an increase in wickedness and its promotion around the globe.

For context of what may be ahead, let's look back at the twentieth century.

It was not only the "charismatic century" with the most Holy Spirit activity and most gospel advancement since the first century. It was also the bloodiest, darkest century in human history.

Entire people groups were nearly wiped out by genocide. Two World Wars claimed nearly 100 million lives. The dark impacts of communism on Russia, China, and other nations claimed tens of millions of others. Totalitarian regimes caused hundreds of millions to groan under surveillance, torture, and oppression. Abortion went from being unusual to state-sponsored, leading to hundreds of millions of deaths in the womb. And yet, as technology increases exponentially, we fear the rise of greater evils in our day. Already, China has concentration camps equipped with modern technology where they imprison religious minorities and dissidents. Chinese residents, constantly surveilled by their phones and billions of cameras, already endure soul-crushing surveillance.

Why would the twentieth century be the greatest century for the cause of Christ, and the greatest century for evil? Why would the rise of an evil in our present day be a sign of a supernatural unity right around the corner?

Two Global Unity Movements

The book of Revelation clearly displays two different unity movements composed of people from every nation.

One is the kingdom of "the Beast." It is given authority over "every tribe and people and language and nation and all who dwell on earth will worship it, everyone whose name has not been written before the foundation of the world in the book of life of the Lamb who was slain" Revelation 13:7-8.

The Beast government marks all its people on the hand or forehead and will not allow buying or selling apart from receiving its mark. Everyone is compelled to worship the Beast.

The great Harlot, Babylon the great, is closely aligned with this united government that rules over the nations. At one point, she is said to be "riding the beast" and making the nations drunk with the wine of sexual immorality.

The Harlot's influence has been visible in every age. Today, her influence is increasing through the championing of LGBT ideology, sexual perversion, hedonism, greed, and control by our national and global elites. Babylon was a unity movement in Genesis 11. It's still pursuing a false unity at the end of the story. And everyone who will not align with her is anathema.

As the Beast and Harlot Babylon rise in power, the book of Revelation shows us a second united body from every tribe, people, language, and nation is also sealed with a mark on their foreheads.[3] This group worships not a beast, but a Lamb. They follow the Lamb wherever He goes. In contrast to Harlot Babylon and her sexual immorality, this unity movement is a pure and spotless Bride. Revelation sees these two unity movements rising to maturity side-by-side immediately before the Lord's return.

Let's not be discouraged. We can expect increasing wickedness and a counterfeit unity movement to arise side-by-side with growing righteousness and the fulfillment of John 17. The seed of God and the seed of the enemy, both wheat and tares, will mature side-by-side.[4]

Sign 4: Declining Denominational Loyalty and the Rise of Networks

If you had asked an American Christian for their religion in 1900, the vast majority would have replied with their denominational affiliation: Methodist, Lutheran, Episcopal, Catholic, Presbyterian.

---

3   Revelation 7 and 14
4   Matthew 13:24-30, The parable of the wheat and the tares is in the context of the end of the age and so is very relevant to our expectation of that time period.

Try the same question today and the vast majority will tell you: "I'm a Christian."

The power of denominationalism has steadily declined for more than a century. Denominational labels mean little to most modern believers.

Even between Catholics, Protestants, and Eastern Orthodox Christians, the three great divisions in the church, there is growing openness to fellowship and partnership. In the United States, Catholics often find Evangelicals as their strongest allies on social issues. Evangelicals are happy to promote devout Catholics for political office or positions of national influence. Charismatic Christians season almost all denominations and experience a unity brought about by a common experience of the Holy Spirit, not by an ecclesiastical hierarchy.

At the same time divisions between denominations are growing weaker, divisions within denominations between conservative and liberal factions are becoming more intense. A Bible-believing United Methodist has more in common with a devout Roman Catholic than with theological liberals in their own denomination.

We are also seeing new types of ecclesial structures emerge, grow, and flourish. While it contains many different groups, Spirit-empowered churches taken together are the second largest Christian body and by far the fastest-growing segment of the global church.[5]

Massive networks of house-churches are spreading like wildfire in the Middle East and Asia. Forced underground by persecution and modeled on the house-to-house worship style of the early church, Discipleship Making Movements (DMMs) are outpacing population

---

5   Data from The Center for the Global Study of Christianity at Gordon-Conwell on modern Pentecostalism. "Spirit empowered" churches make up more than 25% of the global church and are the fastest growing segment. Available at: https://www.gordonconwell.edu/wp-content/uploads/sites/13/2024/01/Status-of-Global-Christianity-2024.pdf

growth and advancing the gospel in closed nations like China and regions like the Middle East with oppositional and oppressive governments.

Here's the bottom line: More than ever before, Christians do not care what denomination you are a part of. They want to know: are you following Jesus?

This represents a massive shift over the past hundred years, one that we fail to notice because it has become normal for us.

Sign 5: More of the Spirit, More of the Word

John 17 unity is a work of the Holy Spirit.

"See how they love one another," marveled the watching pagan world at the first century church. Love is always the greatest sign of the Spirit.

However, the early church was also known for signs and wonders, generosity, sacrificial compassion, and bold testimony. All of these are also works of the Holy Spirit. Peter, speaking about the church age, says it is a fulfillment of Joel 2:28: "In the last days, I will pour out my Spirit on all people…"

For much of church history, gifts of the Spirit like speaking in tongues, prophecy, and miracles were incredibly rare, and the progress of the gospel was slow. Since the first modern case of speaking in tongues in 1901, we've seen an explosion of the gifts immeasurably larger than what happened in the first century. The Pentecostal-charismatic movement along with global mission movements have brought all of these elements back to the forefront of the normal Christian experience. The result has been the rapid expansion of the gospel around the globe.

John 17 unity also requires us to be "sanctified in the truth." To be maturely one, we must be "washed by the Word."[6] Along with the

---

6   Ephesians 5:26

increase in the Spirit's presence, we are also seeing access to God's Word increase as never before. The proliferation of audio recordings of the Bible through small, electronic devices is giving even the illiterate access to the Word of God. Translation movements are partnering together and rapidly closing in on zero Bible-less peoples. Many mature teaching voices open the word with wisdom, blessing the entire Body of Christ. Radio, TV, and the internet ensure every person with a mobile phone can access the word of God with ease. Our modern situation makes it hard to imagine the Middle Ages, where many Christian towns did not have even one Bible.

John 17 unity requires an abundance of the Spirit of God and the Word of God. There has never been more access to the Spirit and the Word in all recorded history.

Sign 6: The Global Prayer and Worship Movement

God moves in response to the cry of His people.[7] Jesus gets what He prays for. But so does His Bride!

What we pray today, God will do tomorrow. Perhaps the biggest indicator that we are approaching the fulfillment of John 17 is the rise of the global prayer and worship movement. Since the turn of the twenty-first century, ministries and movements prioritizing worship and prayer have rapidly expanded globally. The concept of 24/7 prayer, a historical footnote prior to the year 2000, has taken off, with hundreds of 24/7 prayer rooms springing up and thousands of other communities inspired to increase their level of prayer and worship.

These global prayer movements, partnering together loosely through decentralized networks and relational connections, are mobilizing tens of millions to pray in one accord. It's as though the Holy Spirit is

---

7 Exodus 2:23-24

gathering His church into a global upper room. The level and quality of prayer in the Body of Christ has never been higher.

The praying church is passionate about God's Word. They are praying for the fulfillment of the Great Commission, for the salvation of the Jewish people, for the outpouring of the Holy Spirit, and for the John 17 unity of the Church. If God is raising up such a movement in our generation, we should expect to see Him answer their cry, in this generation or the next.

Sign 7: Increasing Unity and Unity Movements

Recently, I facilitated a gathering of church leaders from around the northeastern United States. As fifty or so leaders from different networks and denominations ministered to the Lord with worship and prayer for several hours, there was a powerful and sweet sense of God's presence and a tangible measure of John 17 unity. God began to speak prophetically, releasing encouragement. The gifts and fruit of the Spirit were in operation and a sweet sense of love, joy, and peace filled our gathering. After a meal together and sharing updates from around the region, we went to our homes with full hearts.

This group, known as the New England Alliance, has been meeting for years. I've been involved since 2007. And since then, we've had dozens of gatherings like this one, characterized by a sense of John 17 unity that seems to grow year after year. This has led to more ministry partnerships around our region than I could recount. Really, I don't know most of what God does through our times together. I can just tell He really enjoys it when we come together and minister to Him.

Similar city-wide, national, and global unity movements are thriving all over the world.

In 2004, when I realized God was calling me be part of the answer to

Jesus's prayer in John 17, I had never met anyone with a similar calling. Today, I've met hundreds of people who believe God has called them to work for the fulfillment of Jesus's prayer. This growth in unity callings is significant because God partners with His people in everything He does. If God is calling people to work for the fulfillment of John 17 unity, it's a sign: He is preparing to do it.

The Signs Align

The church today is increasingly global, multi-lingual, and interconnected and decreasingly denominational. For the first time in history, we are closing in on the fulfillment of the Great Commission. We can reasonably hope this will occur within the next decade or two. We are incredibly close to adding "every tribe, and every language" to our ranks. We are experiencing growing evil and persecution but manifesting the power of the Spirit and the Word of God in fresh measure. The Church has a growing prayer movement that is crying out for an answer to Jesus's prayer. It also has many unity movements that are growing in quantity and quality.

Many of the preconditions for Jesus's prayer to be answered have fallen into place before our eyes or seem to be just over the horizon.

While no one knows for sure, it is possible, even likely, there are people alive today who will see a complete fulfillment of Jesus's prayer. I think if it is not in my lifetime, my children or grandchildren will witness it. However, we must be careful, remembering that our vision is partial and narrow. Whether we are the generation that sees it in fullness, or simply a steppingstone on the way to perfect unity, the pursuit of Jesus's dream is worth it.

But what might the final fulfillment look like? And how will we recognize the answer to Jesus's prayer when it arrives?

7

The Fullness

For two and a half weeks in February 2023, the tiny town of Asbury, Kentucky, experienced a remarkable outpouring of the Spirit. In that brief window of time, an estimated 160,000 people descended on the small city of about 7,000. Asbury was overwhelmed and nearly shut down by the sudden influx.

The attraction was simple: the presence of God manifesting in a continual, spontaneous worship service at Asbury College. Many made personal commitments to Jesus Christ, others were reconciled, healed, saved, and delivered. Still others performed acts of radical generosity. The grace of God was available to all in an unusual way.

One of my favorite testimonies came from a friend of mine. As he worshipped in the chapel, he looked around the room and saw several famous Christian musicians and celebrities. And yet, no one was paying attention to them, and they weren't looking for attention. Everyone's eyes were focused on the Lamb who was slain. He was the one, the only one who could command attention and worship. He was the only attraction.

The outpouring came off with evident humility and meekness. I can't name a single person who started it or ran it, although many people were involved and used of God in leadership. The outpouring sparked many other similar moves around the globe, including some that are still worshipping 24/7. An unusual sense of unity was experienced by participants.

This move of God, with no preparation, planning, or promotion, brought tens of thousands together in one place and touched hundreds of millions of people around the globe through social media. As we attempt to look into the future and imagine what the fullness of John 17 might look like, the Asbury outpouring is an intriguing modern case study.

John 17: A Matter of Grace

In 2013, while I was walking to a prayer meeting in Boston, God asked me a question:

"Do you want to know how I'm going to pull it off?"

Immediately, I knew what the Lord was asking me. He wanted to tell me how He would answer Jesus's prayer. The funny thing was, while I believed He would do it, I had never asked Him how it would happen. I simply believed because Jesus prayed it.

"Show me," I responded.

Immediately, I saw a very large bathroom sink made of crystal-clear glass. It was clearly a hand-washing sink, and yet its size was much larger than a normal sink, closer in size to a bathtub. The basin had a number of objects in it that you'd find in a bathtub if you have small children: plastic boats, a rubber duck, and other floating toys. At a certain point, an invisible hand turned on the water. The crystal-clear basin began to fill up and the many objects in the basin all began to rise with the water level.

Interpretation

All at once, I knew what the Lord was saying.

John 17 unity is a grace gift, or an anointing that the Lord was waiting to pour out. When He begins to pour it out, it will cause everyone in the Church to rise together—the new believer and the mature saint alike would all rise to the same level of unity through this gift of God's grace. Water and the bathroom sink are symbolic of how this outpouring of grace will bring holiness and the washing of the Word, leading to purity.

He said to me: "The crystal-clear glass basin represents a purified and refined leadership."

I knew this was essential to God's plan—if the basin was cracked or had any imperfection, the water would have quickly leaked out on the floor. While I didn't realize it right away, this vision aligns well with Paul's vision of mature unity in Ephesians 4. The five-fold leadership gifts have a significant role to play in bringing the church into the unity of the faith. They are the basin that contains mature unity.

But let's not miss the main point: an outpouring of a special grace-gift for unity through the Holy Spirit is God's plan to answer John 17 in full. It's that simple. We are just waiting for everything to be ready and the Father to turn on the faucet, releasing the crystal clear water that will unite us in perfect love. We are waiting for the best wine, saved for last.

From Partial Fulfillments to Complete Fulfillment

The Asbury outpouring is a modern example of a measure of John 17 unity being poured out, suddenly and unexpectedly. This outpouring, along with many other similar experiences in Church history, is a partial fulfillment of Jesus's prayer. People who came to Asbury experienced a divine union with God and with one another by the power of the Holy Spirit. The glory of Jesus, the manifestation of the Spirit that makes the Father and Son one and makes us one, was certainly present (John 17:22).

We could look at other historical examples of partial fulfillments to Jesus's prayer. But, there is an entire book of the Bible that documents the Father's initial response to the prayer of His Son.

Let's read the book of Acts in light of John 17.

Partial Fulfillment: The Book of Acts

In Acts chapter 2, we see the Father's first salvo, His first significant move to answer Jesus's prayer.

> "When the day of Pentecost came, they were all together in one place. Suddenly a sound like the blowing of a violent wind came from heaven and filled the whole house where they were sitting. They saw what seemed to be tongues of fire that divided and came to rest on each of them. All of them were filled with the Holy Spirit and began to speak in other tongues as the Spirit enabled them." Acts 2:1-4

Glory

God immediately fills the believers with the Spirit, manifested externally with visible, divided flames of fire on their heads. He also manifests the coming of the Spirit with a great rushing wind from heaven.

The rushing in of God's glory with visible fire parallels how God came to dwell in Moses's Tabernacle and Solomon's Temple.[1] Now God's people are the Temple. Now God lives not in a house, but in His

---

1 See Exodus 40 (Moses's Tabernacle) and 2 Chronicles 5 (Solomon's Temple) for the Old Testament parallels to Acts 2:1-4.

people. To further drive home this connection, we were told earlier that there were about 120 people in the upper room. Solomon's Temple was 120 cubits in height, and there were 120 Levitical Priests present when the glory of God entered the temple, preventing them from ministering to God.

This time, however, the priesthood of 120 are enabled to minister, sharing the word of God with boldness. The people of God have become the temple of God.

The Father is doing exactly what Jesus prayed in John 17:22—He is pouring out the glory of Jesus: "The glory that you gave me I am giving to them, so that they may be one just as we are one."

The Undoing of Babel

> "Now there were staying in Jerusalem God-fearing Jews from every nation under heaven. When they heard this sound, a crowd came together in bewilderment, because each one heard their own language being spoken. Utterly amazed, they asked: 'Aren't all these who are speaking Galileans? Then how is it that each of us hears them in our native language? Parthians, Medes and Elamites; residents of Mesopotamia, Judea and Cappadocia, Pontus and Asia, Phrygia and Pamphylia, Egypt and the parts of Libya near Cyrene; visitors from Rome (both Jews and converts to Judaism); Cretans and Arabs—we hear them declaring the wonders of God in our own tongues!'" Acts 2:5-11.

The first manifestation of the Spirt is a supernatural ability to speak in other languages. The outpouring of the Spirit is a reversal of the futility of Babel. At Babel, God scattered the nations and confused their language. But, on Pentecost, God begins to reunite humanity, enabling us to understand "the wonders of God in our own language." At Babel, the pursuit of glory and fame in false unity led to confusion. Now, the Son's humble obedience brings God's glory to earth. The nations are reunited back to the Creator with a common language, and a common Spirit.

The nations,[2] here represented by Jews and Jewish proselytes from the dispersion, are beginning to be regathered in answer to Jesus's prayer. The futility and confusion of Babel is undone.

Harvest

> "When the people heard this, they were cut to the heart and said to Peter and the other apostles, 'Brothers, what shall we do?' Peter replied, 'Repent and be baptized, every one of you, in the name of Jesus Christ for the forgiveness of your sins. And you will receive the gift of the Holy Spirit. The promise is for you and your children and for all who are far off—for all whom the Lord our God will call.' With many other words he warned them; and he pleaded with them, 'Save yourselves from this corrupt generation.' Those who accepted his message were baptized, and about three thousand were added to their number that day." Acts 2:37-41.

Pentecost was a feast that celebrated both the first harvest and the giving of the Law on Mt. Sinai. The outpouring of the Spirit leads to a great harvest. When the Law was given and Israel worshipped the golden calf, 3,000 were killed on the same day.[3] Now, 3,000 are saved as the Spirit is poured out, the new law, written on human hearts (Jer. 31:31).

---

2   This catalogue of nations in Acts 2 is a direct reference to the seventy nations of Genesis 10 and the division of languages in Genesis 11.

3   Exodus 32:28

In this initial harvest, we see yet another answer to Jesus's prayer. The pouring out of His Spirit of love and glory binds the 120 together as one. Just as John 17:23 predicts, their union causes the unbelieving world to recognize that Jesus is the Son of God. Three thousand new believers now worship Him as Lord, including those who just fifty days before participated in killing the Messiah.

From Outpouring to a New Normal

The unity of the early church is legendary:

> "They devoted themselves to the apostles' teaching and to fellowship, to the breaking of bread and to prayer. Everyone was filled with awe at the many wonders and signs performed by the apostles. All the believers were together and had everything in common. They sold property and possessions to give to anyone who had need. Every day they continued to meet together in the temple courts. They broke bread in their homes and ate together with glad and sincere hearts, praising God and enjoying the favor of all the people. And the Lord added to their number daily those who were being saved." Acts 2:42-47

Out of the power encounter of Pentecost Sunday comes a new normal that is incarnated by the early church in the midst of daily life.

Is there a better description of the practical, day-to-day experience of living in unity than this? It's all the Marxists dreamed of, "from each according to his ability, to each according to his need," but completely voluntary and freely offered (and without the 100 million dead bodies that Marxism produced). The outpouring of the Spirit in a moment of glory leads to a new normal, a community where miracles are common, radical generosity is the norm, worship, prayer, and communion are central, and joyful simplicity permeates. This is the most beautiful description of an ideal human community in all of literature.

Only the Opening Salvo

The events of Acts 2 are without a doubt the Father's opening salvo, His initial response to Jesus's prayer. All the elements of John 17 are present. There's an outpouring of the Spirit that fills the church with glory. Unbelievers witness it, recognize Jesus is the Son of God, repent, and are baptized (John 17:23). Other unbelievers also recognize Jesus and are stirred to oppose and persecute the church.

This outpouring of glory, a momentary explosion of the power of God, leads to a new normal for the community that is characterized by the Word of God, warm fellowship, communion, and prayer. Believers love one another and sell their possessions to give to each other. They lay down their lives to love one another, living out Jesus's new commandment in John 13:34-35.

However, Acts 2 is only the beginning of a pattern that will repeat throughout the book of Acts. It is not one and done. The Father has just begun to respond to His Son's dying request.

The Five Outpourings of Acts

The book of Acts records five different outpourings of the Spirit. They follow the pattern of Jesus's parting command for the disciples to be his witnesses, "In Jerusalem, in all Judea and Samaria, and to the ends of the earth."

Each successive salvo is yet another strategic, powerful response from the Father in answer to the prayer of Jesus.

In Acts 4:28-31 the Holy Spirit is poured out again on the apostles in Jerusalem as they pray for boldness in response to persecution. Once

Chapter 7: The Fullness

again, a natural manifestation, the shaking of their prayer room, is accompanied by a fresh filling of the Holy Spirit. Following the pattern of Acts 2, a fresh manifestation of unity expressed in a "new normal" follows the outpouring of the Spirit, along with boldness, power, and generosity.

> "All the believers were one in heart and mind. No one claimed that any of their possessions was their own, but they shared everything they had. With great power the apostles continued to testify to the resurrection of the Lord Jesus. And God's grace was so powerfully at work in them all that there were no needy persons among them. For from time to time those who owned land or houses sold them, brought the money from the sales and put it at the apostles' feet, and it was distributed to anyone who had need." Acts 4:32-35

In Acts 8:15-17, the Holy Spirit is poured out on non-Jews for the first time, on Samaritans. In this instance, rather than a sovereign outpouring in response to prayer, the emphasis is on how the Spirit came by the laying on of the apostles' hands. Out of this encounter in Samaria, the gospel begins its journey to the ends of the earth, as Philip the Evangelist brings a high official of Ethiopia into the family of God. The nations are beginning to become one in the Messiah.

In Acts 10, Peter is shocked as the Holy Spirit is sovereignly poured out on Cornelius and other uncircumcised Gentiles. This unexpected development led to a conference of Jewish leaders in Jerusalem, where they wrestled with the fact that God was granting salvation even to the nations.

This outpouring led to a new normal once again, where Gentile believers are now fully included as members of the Body of Christ. And the inclusion of the nations leads to a fresh explosion of missions. In

Antioch, a mixed company of Jewish and Gentile believers experience the same fellowship in the Spirit as in Acts 2, but with a fresh manifestation of the missionary spirit. By Acts 13, we see Paul and Barnabas sent out to bring the gospel to the ends of the earth.

Finally, in Acts 19:6, the Holy Spirit is poured out at "the ends of the earth" on twelve Greeks in Ephesus. It is no coincidence that that this outpouring precedes the most miraculous recorded period of Paul's ministry, the downfall of witchcraft and pagan worship with thousands of sorcery scrolls being burnt, and the founding of one of the strongest early churches. After this outpouring, within two years, all of modern-day Turkey hears the good news. This fifth outpouring leads to unprecedented growth and harvest.

The five outpourings of Acts follow a similar pattern. As the gospel spreads into new territory and new nations, there are periodic, fresh outpourings of the Holy Spirit, leading to periods of a "new normal" characterized by unity, generosity, the miraculous, and new missionary expansion to the unreached parts of the earth.

The relationship between moments of outpouring, like Pentecost or Asbury, and the "new normal" periods, like Acts 2:42-47 is significant. God does not pour out His glory in a constant, sustained way. Imagine how different the story would be if the intensity of Acts 2:1-4 were sustained throughout the entire book. Instead, He pours out His Spirit in waves that come regularly, periodically. We might think of the moments of outpouring as the crests of the wave, where the power is most intense.

The Father's Plan

In Acts, we can clearly see how the Father's plan to answer Jesus' prayer unfolded over a period of about thirty years. I think it is biblically consistent to see this not only as His plan in Acts, but for the entire church age. This is His plan to fulfill John 17.

He is sending glorious outpourings of the Holy Spirit. The Spirit does not come all at once, but in waves. Each wave leads into a new normal, where believers are meant to pour out to one another what they've received (fellowship, generosity, gifts of the Spirit) and pour out to the world (missions, miracles, evangelism). In these periods, God also tests the church, allowing circumstances and persecution to refine His people. Some, like Barnabas, pass the test and are approved for future service. Others fail the test, like Ananias and Saphira.

As we ask for and anticipate a full answer to Jesus's prayer, we should keep the pattern of Acts in mind. Waves of glory, followed by seasons where we walk in a new normal, where we pour out to one another and share with world what the Father has poured into us.

If the pattern of Acts is predictive of how God intends to ultimately answer the prayer of Jesus, we can expect outpourings of the Spirit to come in waves, over and over again, interspersed with more normal periods, until the whole world hears the gospel, and the church is perfectly one. We can expect these waves to become more frequent and intense as we approach the fullness of John 17 unity and ultimately, the return of the Lord.

Seven Marks of a Complete Fulfillment of John 17

If the fulfillments in the book of Acts are only partial answers to John 17, what will complete fulfillment look like? Here are seven marks of a complete fulfillment of Jesus's prayer.

Global in Scope

As we have seen, Jesus's prayer is closely tied to God's overall plan for the nations and Israel. A complete fulfillment must include people from every tribe, language, people and nation, including an Israeli remnant. The fullness of John 17 requires a truly global family of believers. John 17:23 and Matthew 28:18-20, the Great Commission, can never be separated.

A Divine Degree of Union

A complete fulfillment must result in a divinely intense union among believers that would satisfy "just as we are one." We are most likely looking for successive outpourings like Acts 2:1-4 but on a global scale, and with a much greater intensity of glory, followed by periods of new normal like in Acts 2:42-47, but with even greater love. If the pattern of Acts is predictive, we can expect this glory to come in waves that grow and escalate with intermediate periods where we walk out the new normal.

Holiness

Unity is corporate holiness. We would expect the people walking in John 17 unity to have an exceptional personal and corporate righteousness. The anointing for John 17 unity from God will contain supernatural empowerment for righteousness that is currently alien to us. The Holy Spirit is the Spirit of holiness.

Maturity

Jesus is the model of what maturity looks like. We would expect this John 17 community to walk in a similar level of faith and confidence in God, miraculous power, intimacy with God, humility, and wisdom that Jesus had when He was on earth. The Jerusalem church in Acts 2-4 is an excellent starting point. We should envision something similar, but far greater in scope, power, generosity, and love. This will be a church that is mature in wisdom, love, and fruit of the Spirit, as well as in signs and wonders and the power of God.

Truth, Doctrine, and Practice

The unity of the Spirit is also unity in truth, just as Jesus prayed, "…sanctify them in truth." We would expect a church walking in John 17 unity to have doctrinal agreement on major issues with diversity in the expression and manifestation of those truths, similar to the unity and diversity of the books of the Bible. The practice of the church will continue to be very diverse from culture to culture, and tradition to tradition, as unity does not mean uniformity. However, there will be doctrinal agreement on central truths.

Leadership

We can expect united leadership to emerge for the global church like what happened in the Acts church. We don't know how this will happen, but we can expect a united, recognized leadership will be at work as described in Ephesians 4.

The Proof of Union

How do we know if we are seeing the fullness of what Jesus prayed for?

When it happens, "the world will know that you [Father] sent me and that you love them [my disciples] even as you love me."

This has happened partially millions of times in history, just as Jesus said, "by this all men will know you are my disciples, when you love one another."

However, the ultimate fulfillment will produce a weight of testimony so great that no one on earth can deny Jesus is the Son of God.

Partial answers to John 17 produce salvation and persecution from the world. Salvation as people recognize Jesus and surrender to His Lordship. Persecution as people recognize Jesus and nonetheless resist His Lordship. The fullness of John 17 will produce such a testimony that the whole world will know and understand who Jesus is.

Pressure and Persecution

As the grace increases, we can expect global persecution to also increase. Some believers will fall away, but others will persevere and increase in holy love for the Lamb of God. Persecution will also drive away false brothers, creating unity by subtraction, as any social advantage of being a believer disappears, and the martyrdom of the saints inspires greater devotion to Jesus and love for one another among those who remain.

As the love of many grows cold due to increasing wickedness, the love of the saints will grow white-hot, to levels not seen in history.

Envisioning Perfect Unity

What if outpourings like Asbury become more common and more widespread? What if God began to release more grace for union with greater regularity and intensity?

We could imagine waves of outpouring coming in regular rhythms and seasons that release revelation of the love of God into the hearts of the saints, followed by less intense seasons where the love of God and unity in the body finds expression through normal church life as we practice love for one another.

In these times of outpouring, impacting billions around the globe, the eyes of the world will be transfixed: "See how they love one another!" Meanwhile, in the more normal rhythms of life, everyday believers who have become "one as the Father and Son are one" will manifest

John 17 unity to unbelievers one-on-one, at work, on the street, in the marketplace, and online.

As Jesus begins to pour out His glory, the glory that makes us one, and this outpouring of grace touches believers from every tribe, language, nation, and people, we will hear the world confess: "Truly, Jesus is the Son of God. Truly, God has loved these people as He loved His own Son, Jesus." John 17:23

This manifestation of perfect unity in the middle of increasing evil will be what draws in the final harvest and may be what ultimately moves the Jewish people to jealousy, leading them to confess, "Blessed is He who comes in the name of the Lord."[4]

A Sign of the End of the Age

Ultimately, the mature expression of John 17 unity, where we are "one as the Father and Son are one" is so powerful, we must think of it as a pre-eschatological sign. In other words, it is such a powerful and historic marker that the Lord will return shortly after we see this glorious promise fulfilled in His people. It is John 17 grace that will make us "pure and spotless and without wrinkle," and "prepared as a Bride for her Husband." If you are alive during the ultimate fulfillment of John 17, "look up, for your redemption is near."

It's difficult to know how far before Jesus's return the Father will answer Jesus's prayer. Here are three imaginative scenarios that are possible from Scripture.

Scenario 1: Perfect Unity, Immediate Return
(Revelation 19, Matthew 24, Revelation 1, 1 Cor. 15)
Waves of glory have beautified, and waves of persecution have battered the church of Jesus Christ. However, after enduring a time of trouble

---
4   Matt. 23:39

not seen since the earth was formed, the Bride of Jesus Christ has emerged a victorious, uncountable multitude from every tribe, nation, and language.

As the Father releases the final wave of grace to the church on earth, Jesus, sitting to His right, gazes at the Father, and with fiery love to His eyes, He says, "It is done. She is perfectly one."

No sooner has this happened than the Father sends Him forth from His right hand: "Go, Receive your Bride." The wedding of the Lamb has finally come. As the Father sends the Son, the church on earth and in heaven, together in one accord cries out, "Come, Lord Jesus."

As unrepentant humanity cries out in mourning, confessing Jesus is King of Kings and Lord of Lords, His victory procession pierces the sky. Accompanied by the host of heaven, He has come to rescue His pure and spotless Bride and bring righteousness at last to the earth.

Scenario 2: Perfect Unity before the Great Tribulation (Revelation 13-14)

The nations have been united under the Beast, seduced by His consort, Harlot Babylon. Technologically-powered control limits the ability of all to buy and sell. Those who refuse to bend the knee suffer surveillance, oppression, torture, and death.

And yet, in the midst of it the worst trouble in human history, the first-fruits of the Lamb have come forth in complete holiness and John 17 unity. The church, perfected in unity, begins to sing and prophesy the glory of the Lamb and the downfall of Babylon, in every human language. The global church perseveres in a state of perfected unity throughout the great tribulation, causing the entire world to know who Jesus is. Some repent and join them, while others reject and persecute them, killing many. Through the midst of this time of darkness, the church remains perfectly one, shining brightly, until the Lord returns.

Scenario 3: The Great Commission and Perfect Unity in the Final Generation

It happened on a Sunday. The last tribe on earth, somewhere in the mountains of the Himalayas, received the gospel in their own language and responded. While no one on earth knew what had happened, the event was recorded in Heaven. The end goal of 2,000 years of missions and the answer to trillions of prayers set off a chain reaction.

Every tribe and language were now in the family. Angels were dispatched to places prepared in advance before the earth was made. The hour had finally come.

Coordinated by prophetic voices on earth under the direction of the Spirit, many of God's people were gathering in extended, Acts 1-style prayer meetings, just like the first disciples had done, but in tens of thousands of locations around the globe. The upper room is global now. As they gathered and prayed, "Let us be one," the Father answered their prayer in fullness. He poured out the best wine, saved for last, on all of His people. He finally released the full measure of glory that makes us one just as He and the Son are one.

The fulfillment of Jesus's prayer had come, and now no one could deny who Jesus was. Men and women either repented or violently opposed the vibrant, holy church.

Just as the day of Pentecost happened about forty years before the judgment on Jerusalem,[5] so this outpouring of John 17 unity started a countdown to the return of the Lord. The generation that saw this union knew they would see His coming, unless they died a martyr's death. The clock was in motion and would not be stopped.

---

5   In Matthew 24, the destruction of Jerusalem in A.D. 70 is closely linked to the return of the Lord even though they are thousands of years apart. Clearly, these events are very similar and there is likely a strong parallel between the first generation of believers, from Acts 2 to the destruction of Jerusalem, and the final generation of believers before the Lord returns.

In this scenario, where the fulfillment of John 17 happens thirty to forty years before the coming of the Lord, an entire generation would grow up in an atmosphere of John 17 unity. They would never know anything different. John 17 unity would be normal Christianity for them.

In Conclusion

The fulfillment of John 17 may closely map onto one of these scenarios, borrow from all of them, or look nothing like this. The people on one side of a spiritual revolution often have false concepts about the other side. We prophesy in part.

However, we can certainly conclude that John 17 will be fulfilled before Jesus returns, and that the fullness will be closely associated in time with His coming. Once this happens, He is not far behind, whether that means a few moments, a few years, or a generation.

While these imaginings may be far from what actually happens, I find envisioning what may come with specificity fills our hearts with faith and hope.

Without a doubt, Jesus is going to get what He prayed for. We can see many indications that history is approaching that moment. And the answer to His prayer may well look something like what we have imagined here.

Part 3: In Pursuit: Seeking the Fullness of John 17

How should we pursue the fullness of John 17?
What personal and corporate mindsets and practices are essential for divine unity?

1

Extraordinary Prayer

In 2004, I had a vision that changed the course of my life.

During an extended season of prayer, I sensed God directing me to call His people to ten days of fasting, repentance and mourning. I saw a vision of a city that had stopped everything. Normal life had come to a screeching halt. Instead of work and play, people were seeking God with prayer, worship, and desperate repentance. For a ten-day period, it was as though the throne room in Heaven had descended on this city. It was covered by a thick, golden hued cloud. I knew this city would never be the same.

As the vision continued, I felt a question rise within me for God: "Is this how you want to answer Jesus's prayer in John 17?" I did not receive an answer, but that question has come to define my purpose in life.

If God's people will stop everything to pray, repent, and wait on the Lord, will we see the fullness of John 17 unity?

I'm still running the experiment.

Although the vision was life-changing and compelling, it did not come with an instruction manual. I threw myself into the pursuit of it, and while I saw much fruit, I also made a lot of serious mistakes.[1]

---

1   If you're interested in learning more, I've written about it in another book, *10 Days: The Unlikely Story of a Global Movement Mourning for the Return of Jesus.*

In 2007, after a number of false starts, I was able to organize a prayer retreat that looked something like the vision God had given me. For ten entire days, all we did was spend time in prayer and worship. While it wasn't a whole city, for the first time in my life, a group of people was doing what I had seen in the vision. This gathering was my first experience of John 17 unity.[2]

> As the first several days rolled along, something incredible and difficult to describe was happening…Supernatural love and unity in the Spirit were happening all around us. God had dropped a taste of John 17 unity on our gathering…Our core group was diverse denominationally, ethnically, in age, and economic background. And yet, all of us noticed the unusual love for one another and unity that God was pouring out. We began talking about it as something we could protect and guard and thinking about how we could honor one another above ourselves. Love and good deeds flowed naturally from this place and all our conversation seemed to be focused on the Lord. Something incredible was happening…
>
> For years I had marveled at Jesus's words, "Let them be one just as we are one." How could human beings experience the type of union that the Father and Son experience *with one another?* But now, we were not just reading about it, we were experiencing a measure of it firsthand. This was something else altogether—it was like heaven on earth.
>
> I like testimonies that can be easily communicated. Healings are like that—someone has a broken bone, people pray, and it is healed. This is very easy to talk about. On the other hand, it's difficult to describe what

---

2   From *10 Days: The Unlikely Story of a Global Movement Mourning for the Return of Jesus*

it is like to experience John 17 unity. I'll do my best.

First of all, it's something inside of you and it's also something around you, in the air. It's in you and it's in the atmosphere. This lines up with Jesus's words in John 17:22 about the key role that His glory plays in unity. His glory is within us through the Holy Spirit, but also all around us.

This experience of glory is between you and God vertically, but it's also between you and other people horizontally. It's the presence of God experienced vertically and horizontally at the same time.

It feels like all you can think about or talk about is Jesus. During those times, one of the things I noticed was that what we often consider normal conversation was almost non-existent. God was doing so much and people could not stop talking about Him.

I was completely surprised by the inner experience of my heart and mind. "Why do I irrationally love all of these people?" I kept asking myself. And yet, I did love them, deeply and from the heart.

It was almost traumatic to move from this dynamic experience of love and glory into what we often call normal life. I had to run out for supplies at one point during the 10 Days; the routine act of going to a local drugstore felt painful. I'd compare it to culture shock—what I had previously considered normal now seemed like spiritual oppression and darkness that was almost too much to bear. In the future, I would learn to carry what I was experiencing along with me, but those initial experiences were a look into the darkness of our world that we simply accept.

Finally, John 17 manifesting resulted in all kinds of love,

good deeds, and miracles in the community. There were too many amazing things happening around us to record it all, but our love for one another was foundational, like a basin that was holding all that God was pouring out on us.

I have never been the same since this experience.

Since that first taste of John 17 unity in 2007, I've participated in dozens of other ten-day prayer gatherings and I've helped spark thousands around the world.[3] I've been involved in houses of prayer on a weekly basis. And, I've participated in many gatherings of leaders where communion with the Lord is our primary goal.

This is what I've witnessed: when we make Jesus the center of our gatherings, He is faithful to show up. And when He shows up through the power of the Holy Spirit, He makes us one in ways we can hardly imagine possible.

If you want to see an increase in John 17 unity, devote yourself to extraordinary prayer and worship with other believers. Make His presence your priority. Nothing unites us like the presence of God.

What Only God Can Do

James 2:15-16 says,

> "If a brother or sister is poorly clothed and lacking in daily food, and one of you says to them, 'Go in peace, be warmed and filled,' without giving them the things needed for the body, what good is that?"

Our elder brother James is pointing out the foolishness of faith without works.

---

3 This original vision has sparked a movement called "10 Days." See more at 10days.net.

Chapter 1: Extraordinary Prayer

Saying "go in peace, be warmed, be filled" are types of blessings—prayers invoking God's presence on someone. James is pointing out how silly and harmful it is to pray for someone's need when it's in your power to provide the answer to their need.

In other words, don't pray for something you can do yourself. Don't pray for God to feed your kids. Start cooking. Don't ask the Lord to serve your wife. Go change a diaper. Don't bless the hungry with words. Feed them and they will be blessed.

However, on the other side, James's reasoning is this: we must pray for what we cannot accomplish on our own. The humanly impossible is the proper object of prayer.

This is why James says the poor in this life are rich in faith.[4] The rich can provide for their own necessities and even many luxuries by their own ability. The poor are constantly praying for the very essentials of life, and this leads to an increase in faith.

The proper object of prayer is what we cannot do for ourselves. This is especially true for what God has explicitly told us He wants to happen. Becoming "one as the Father and Son are one" is something that only God can do. I cannot make it happen. You cannot make it happen. We can't pool our resources and make it happen, although it will involve the participation of all believers in a generation.

John 17 unity is something God has revealed He wants. We know when we pray in agreement with Jesus's prayer, we are agreeing with the Father's own desire.

It's something only God can do. It's something God wants to do. And because of that, it is a worthy object of perpetual, unceasing, and fervent prayer until we see the fullness on earth.

---

4   James 2:5

Extraordinary Prayer for Extraordinary Promises

Extraordinary promises from God deserve extraordinary prayer[5] until what is promised becomes reality.

The type and intensity of the prayer should correspond to the request. A quick prayer and band aid for a child with a skinned knee is sufficient. It's a minor matter that will soon pass.

In the case of the fullness of John 17 unity, we are speaking about one of the culminating spiritual events of this age, something closely linked to the Lord's return. We are talking about a prophetic promise of Jesus that is unfulfilled after almost 2,000 years. This is kind of a big deal.

Personally, I make it a habit once a year to take ten days off from work for fasting, repentance, prayer, and worship with other believers.[6] One of the primary goals of these extraordinary times of prayer is John 17 unity.

Time and time again, we see localized breakthroughs in unity in cities that pray together. It seems that faith, hope, and love rise up in regions where the church comes together in extraordinary prayer.

Integrate the Vertical and Horizontal

While John 17 unity is something that only God can do, it's also something He has committed to do in partnership with His people on earth.

Something powerful takes place when we combine the power of prayer for unity, asking God to do what only He can do, with pursuing unity with one another in tangible ways on earth. This could involve

---

[5] The phrase "extraordinary prayer" comes from the great theologian and revivalist Jonathan Edwards, It means an unusual level of prayer—beyond the ordinary.

[6] See 10days.net for more information on how to join in this global gathering of extraordinary prayer.

reaching out to other believers in a city who usually don't work together, reconciling with a brother who has wronged you, or even just inviting other believers over for dinner, fellowship, and worship.

When we combine prayer and action, the vertical and the horizontal, we acknowledge the oneness Jesus prayed for can only come as a gift from heaven, while also recognizing that we are heaven's representatives on earth.

Because the Holy Spirit lives inside other believers, there is less of a difference between the vertical and horizontal dimensions than we often think. Whether we are speaking to God in the heavenly realm or talking to a brother on earth, the Holy Spirit is mediating and empowering our communication—or better yet, our communion.

Somehow, focusing our efforts for unity on prayer makes us more aware of the dimension only God can do. Putting feet to our prayers by working for unity reminds us that we have a role to play as well. When we do both together, we are working as sons and partners of our Father in heaven, peacemakers who walk as Jesus walked in humble dependence and bold confidence in God.

Extraordinary Prayer Increases our Faith

Nothing increases our faith like spending extended times in God's presence. And faith is the very thing we require most if we want to see God's grace come into the world.

> "For by grace you have been saved through faith."
> Ephesians 2:8

> "For in the gospel the righteousness of God is revealed—a righteousness that is by faith from first to last, just as it is written, 'the righteous will live by faith.'"
> Romans 1:17, NIV

The good news about Jesus is by faith from beginning to end. We enter through faith, are sustained by faith, and finish at the end with faith. Biblically speaking, we can imagine faith as a conduit or pipe that allows the power and grace of God in heaven to come to us on earth. After all, the grace of God comes to us "through faith." God is the provider of grace; faith is the pipeline that grace passes through on its way to human beings.

We only access God's grace through faith. We need the grace of God to be saved and to do anything of eternal value. Faith is the only way we can receive this precious resource.

Faith sometimes refers to a general trust in God. However, it can also be applied for the sake of certain specific ends.

For example, the woman who touched the edge of Jesus's garment and received a healing did not just "believe in Jesus" generally, she believed that Jesus would heal the flow of blood that had plagued her for twelve years. Jesus acknowledged her as a person of great faith.

Just as the woman with the flow of blood reached out to Jesus with great faith for her healing, we need to move with similar single-minded desperation for the fulfillment of Jesus's prayer in John 17. We don't just need faith "in God." We need faith for the fullness of John 17 unity.

I am not aware of anything that leads to a greater increase of faith than extended seasons of Scripture-saturated worship and prayer.

Dead Ends: Small Vision, Small Faith

We must diligently avoid setting our aim too low.

A common misunderstanding about John 17 unity is that it means "Christians together in the same room, not fighting." If this is our goal, not much faith and therefore not much prayer will be needed. I've been in many meetings where "being in the same room, not fighting" is the unspoken goal. While I am convinced it is usually better than "being in the same room, fighting," this level of unity bears little resemblance to Jesus's prayer in John 17.

"Being in the same room, not fighting" is a warm, inviting campfire. "Let them be one as we are one" is the searing brilliance of the sun. They're similar in some ways, but light-years apart.

We need to anchor our faith to the fullness of what Jesus prayed—that we would all be one, just as the Father and Son are one. Let's make sure our faith is aimed high enough. And, when we have aimed as high as we can ask, think, or imagine, let's remember with Paul that God's plan is still immeasurably greater.

Faith is an Aligned Life

Once we have anchored ourselves in hope to the glorious promises of God's word, faith means bringing our lives into agreement with the future, aligning ourselves with where we are going.

Imagine that you knew in three years you'd be moving to a foreign nation for work, a place where the culture and language are new to you. In this nation, they despise foreigners who cannot speak their language but honor those who are able to navigate their customs and speak fluently. Your success or failure hinges on learning their language. Wouldn't you want to learn their customs and gain as much fluency as possible before you move?

Similarly, as we look for an answer to Jesus's prayer, we need to bring our lives into alignment with this future state. We need to live life as though we are going there.

Am I making major decisions with this destination as a driving factor? Is my daily life aligned with God's purpose in John 17? Is our family life positioning the next generation to be part of the answer to this prayer? Are my work, my financial decisions, and my closest relationships advancing what Jesus is going to do, or are we at cross-purposes with the Lord? Am I living out the kingdom values that lead to John 17 unity in my local church community?

As we attempt to bring our lives into alignment with our faith confession, we will begin to see and feel just how far we are from the fullness of what Jesus prayed for. Having done all we can, this realization of lack will naturally lead us back to prayer if our hearts remain tender.

When faith cannot reach its goal apart from a miracle, faith moves into prayer, speaking to the mountain to move. Jesus's prayer in John 17 is impossible. Thankfully, our God specializes in turning the impossible into reality.

Treat the Holy Spirit as the Guest of Honor

While faith is the only way to receive God's grace, there is something else, *Someone* else, who is even more important to John 17 unity—the Holy Spirit.

If we are serious in our pursuit of John 17 unity, we must recognize that it is fundamentally a spiritual reality that only comes through the power and person of the Holy Spirit.

Within the Trinity, the Holy Spirit is the perfect bond of love and unity between Father and Son. Likewise, the oneness of the church "as the Father and the Son are one" is made possible through the gift of the Holy Spirit to the church. As the only one who is able bring about this divine miracle, at all costs we must have the Holy Spirit as our guest of honor.

I know of no better way to increase the power and presence of the Holy Spirit in a community than periods of extraordinary prayer and a communal lifestyle of prayer. It is the pattern of Acts. It is the pattern of history. More prayer leads to more of the power and presence of the Holy Spirit.

Dead Ends: Minimize the Holy Spirit for Unity's Sake

The problem with Holy Spirit is that He is often offensive, both to us and others.

I remember some of my earliest experiences with the Holy Spirit in corporate gatherings. People started speaking what seemed to be gibberish, then crying, then laughing at inappropriate times and even rolling around on the ground and falling over.

"Are these people insane?" I wondered.

It seemed like complete chaos to my rational mind. And yet, soon after these things took place, we were experiencing a powerful manifestation of John 17 unity.

"Are these people drunk?" wondered some in the crowd when the Holy Spirit was first poured out in Acts 2. Peter, however, was not embarrassed, nor did he try to minimize the move of the Spirit. Instead, he got up, explained what was happening, and 3,000 were saved.

Then, as now, it is a dead-end to try to minimize the Holy Spirit in our corporate gatherings for the sake of unity. We can't treat Holy Spirit like our embarrassing uncle and expect to receive His blessing. This does not mean our gatherings should be disordered free-for-alls, although if given a choice I would prefer the chaos of the nursery to the bleak serenity of the funeral home.

At the end of the day, if our goal is John 17 unity, the presence of the Holy Spirit must be our priority. Let's not make the mistake of thinking we can have any meaningful unity apart from the Uniter.

Conclusion

I have spent more than twenty years in pursuit of John 17 unity.

In my experience, nothing brings more unity than believers praying and worshipping together in an extraordinary way. It changes our perspective, raises our faith, and attracts the presence of Holy Spirit. Biblically speaking, nothing is more powerful. In the book of Acts, the initial outpouring of the Holy Spirit is preceded by ten days of united prayer. Historically, we almost always see moves of the Spirit preceded by periods of extraordinary prayer. While none of us have experienced the fullness of John 17 unity, and all of us are going somewhere we have never been before, biblically, historically, and experientially, the evidence is clear. Extraordinary prayer is an essential part of God's plan to bring us into complete unity.

2

Spiritual Unity and Structural Unity

In the early 1740s, a great awakening shook the British colonies in America.

From Georgia in the extreme south, a newly settled colony with just over 1,000 inhabitants, to Massachusetts in the north, a young man with a voice like an angel, clad in black robes and a white wig, rode throughout the colonies preaching that men should repent and be saved.[1]

George Whitefield's itinerant ministry throughout the colonies made him the first person to be universally recognizable in American history. Almost all four million inhabitants would hear him speak in person at least once. Preaching every day, many times a day, indoors and outdoors, in heat, cold, rain, and snow, the fields were white for harvest wherever he spoke.

Whitefield was part of an evangelistic renewal movement composed of members of many denominations. While he himself was ordained in the Church of England, he partnered closely with Presbyterians and New England Congregationalists, and he was one of the founders of the Methodist movement. Denominational affiliation was not the most

---

1 See *George Whitefield* by Arnold Dallimore to read more on the life and times of the famed evangelist.

important thing to him, but rather the gospel going forth, the salvation of souls, and a vibrant expression of the Christian faith. Often, he would face the greatest opposition from his own denomination. Anglican leaders were critical of his itinerant ministry, of his methodology, especially his outdoor preaching, and of his partnerships with believers from other denominations.

At one point, he had a telling conversation with a leader of the Anglican church about his partnerships with Christians from different denominations:

> [I, Whitefield] urged that it was best to preach the new birth, and the power of godliness, and not to insist so much on the form: for the people would never be brought to one mind as to that; nor did Jesus Christ ever intend it. "Yes, but He did," said Dr Cutler. "How do you prove it?" "Because Christ prayed 'that all might be one, even as Thou Father and I are One,'" I replied, "That was spoken of the inward union of the souls of believers with Jesus Christ, and not of the outward Church." "That cannot be," said Dr Cutler, "for how then could it be said, 'that the world might know that Thou has sent me'?" [He took] it for granted that the Church of England was the only true apostolic church…[2]

Whitefield uses Jesus's prayer in John 17 as a basis for his partnership with believers from different denominations. He was convinced that cross-denominational partnerships among groups preaching the importance of the new birth were part of the answer to Jesus's prayer in John 17. The Anglican Commissary had a different perspective: His contention was that God would clearly answer Jesus's prayer in John 17. However, this ultimate and complete unity of the faith would take place through the one true Church, the Church of England.

---

2   *George Whitefield, Vol. I* pg. 529

Whitefield went on to say, "I saw regenerate souls among the Baptists, among the Presbyterians, among the Independents, and among the Church [of England] – all children of God, and yet all born again in a different way of worship."[3]

Spiritual vs Structural

Whitefield discerned the Holy Spirit at work cross-denominationally, in a way that was spiritual instead of structural. He saw John 17 being fulfilled outside the boundaries of traditional denominations as believers united to see the lost saved. The Anglican bishops believed John 17 unity would be structural, within the Anglican church, which could trace its founding generationally back to the apostles. The Anglican church was the "one true church," God's true representatives on earth. Therefore, the Anglican church was the key to John 17 unity.

Today, the structural splintering of Christianity has massively accelerated. By some estimates, there are over 45,000 Christian denominations.

However, the question remains: who was right—Whitefield or the Anglican bishops? For Jesus's prayer in John 17 to be answered, do we all need to join in the same church hierarchy? Do we need to be joined in an organizational structure to be one?

Answering the question is critical to how we will pursue John 17 unity. Should we be directing our efforts to drawing people into the Anglican Church (or some other denominational structure), or does God have a different strategy to bring us into perfect union?

Structural Unity[4]

I've known many Anglicans today, and I've never met one who thought

---

3   *George Whitefield, Vol I* page 530.
4   Structural Unity here and throughout refers to organizational, hierarchical, or denominational unity.

John 17 unity would happen through the Anglican church hierarchy. In fact, I'm not aware of a single, mainstream Protestant group that thinks it is the "one true church" and that everyone else needs to join them.[5]

There are several smaller, cult-like denominations that believe salvation only comes through their group and other groups that are more separatist and hesitant to partner. However, most Protestants don't believe their church hierarchy is the "one true church". This mindset, which we might call denominationalism, has greatly declined in the Protestant world.

However, the Roman Catholic Church and Eastern Orthodox Church do make these claims. And, if anyone has a good claim to be "the Church," these two groups have the strongest claims. Their churches are most ancient with credible ties to the first century apostles, and the Roman Catholic church makes up over half of all global Christians.

While these groups acknowledge some people may be saved outside of their church hierarchies, their official teachings look for unity to be manifested within their organizational structures.

Is the future of John 17 unity a return to hierarchical and structural unity within the Roman or Eastern Churches? Or should we aim, as Whitefield claimed, for a spiritual unity among believers who have experienced the new birth?

Can Structural Unity Produce John 17 Unity?

I have tremendous respect for the Roman Catholic and Eastern Orthodox traditions. The lives of the saints on both sides of this schism are a continual inspiration. Orthodoxy has been a deep well for my walk of faith. As a son of the Protestant Reformation, tracing my natural ancestry back to the German reformers, I'm thankful for all that I've learned about God from both traditions.

---

5   With so many denominations, no doubt I am forgetting someone.

As we consider the question, "Is John 17 unity primarily structural?" we must consider the visible fruit of "structural unity."

Are any of these ecclesial structures currently producing unusual love? Are we seeing John 17 unity manifesting to a greater degree in Roman Catholicism or Eastern Orthodoxy? Are the believers from these traditions exhibiting supernatural love for one another and unusual holiness?

While there is value in their structural unity and there are people notable for their holiness among both groups, the answer is clear. We do not see a more mature expression of John 17 unity in either group. In fact, we see the same divisions, heresies, conflicts, and problems in these churches that exist in the broader Protestant world.

If we're not seeing John 17 manifested at a higher level among Roman Catholics or Eastern Orthodox believers, why would we believe that all of us joining these structures would suddenly produce that effect?

Spiritual Unity

No hierarchy, no organization, can ever make us "one as the Father and the Son are one." This degree and intensity of union can only be a work of the Holy Spirit.

This doesn't mean that organizational unity is not important, valuable, and even commanded by God. It is a significant, lower form of unity. However, it's not sufficient to get us to John 17. If tomorrow, all 45,000 Christian denominations miraculously merged into one denomination, we would not suddenly see the fullness of John 17.

What Jesus prays is only possible by an extraordinary work of the Spirit of God, a work that truly is beyond what we could ask or imagine. While structural unity has a role to play, if we want to see John 17 in fullness, we need to focus our pursuit primarily on the unity that comes from the Holy Spirit.

The Body of Christ and the Spirit[6]

Take a moment to become aware of your body. Move your hands and wiggle your toes. Flex your arms and stretch your legs.

What makes something belong to your body? At first, it seems like a very simple question. My arms, my legs, my chest, my organs, my head—all of these are part of my body. But, we might find some grey areas around the edges. Is hair part of my body? I can't control it and when I cut it I feel no pain. How about the billions of bacteria that inhabit your gut and are essential for digestion? How about a dead, outer layer of skin that's about to fall off? Are they part of the body?

While some of these marginal questions may be hard to answer, it's utterly obvious the tree across the yard and the chair you're sitting on are not part of your body. One major indicator is that you can't move them using only your mind as you can move your hands, feet, and head. Another indicator is that you feel nothing when they are struck.

The Bible has a simple, easy-to-understand definition of what constitutes a body: A body is anything that has a living soul in it.[7] Wherever the life, breath, or spirit inside of you can go, that is your body.

The Bible uses the image of the body to speak about the church. However, it is much more than a useful metaphor—it is a fundamental reality. The church is the body of Christ because the Spirit of Christ inhabits the church. Just as our human spirits fill and animate our bodies, even so the Spirit of Christ fills and animates the church. Just

---
6 This paradigm of the "Body of Christ" has been discussed earlier as well. The repetition may be helpful here.
7 Genesis 2:7

as our human minds move and direct our bodies, even so "…we have the mind of Christ."[8]

Having said this, it should be clear: wherever the Spirit of God is, there is the church. And, where the Spirit is absent, the church is absent, even if the external forms of the church are present.

Connecting to the Head

Jesus Christ is the Head of the Body. The head is the part that directs and leads the entire body. If a connection to the head is severed, as in the case of paralysis, that part of the body that is severed can no longer move or function.

While earthly leadership is important for the church, our head is Jesus Christ. Connection to Him is most essential. Having the Holy Spirit, who communicates from Jesus, the head, to us is what makes us part of His body.

However, when we connect to our Head, we also automatically connect to the rest of the Body. In fact, we quite literally connect to the Head through one another. So, our spiritual connection to the Head brings us into connection with every other part, but our spiritual connection to one another also connects us to Christ. Our connection to Christ can never be separated from our connection to one another.

It is a mistake to think that any human organization, hierarchy, or structure, no matter how important or necessary, can substitute for this essential fact: Jesus is the head of the church. Our inclusion in the church is only possible by the Holy Spirit. John 17 unity is a work of the Holy Spirit. And yet, structural unity is still important. After all, the hand connects to the head through the arm. If the arm is cut off,

---

8   1 Corinthains 2:16. Paul explains the body/spirit connection between Christ and the church in depth throughout 1 Corinthians 2.

the hand is also severed. We can only be connected to the head through one another.

While structural unity is significant, it is not sufficient to produce John 17. In a dead body, the hand and arm may still be connected, yet there is no life because the spirit has left the body.

Furthermore, our assumptions about what structural unity looks like may be completely wrong. I don't think anyone still believes, as Anglicans of Whitefield's day did, that John 17 will be fulfilled when everyone joins the Church of England. Perhaps John 17 unity will be more relational, or look more like a network, rather than a top-down organization. There are other ways of being structurally one that do not look like a traditional denomination.

We may not see a way out of our current state of structural division. However, the pathway that Whitefield followed is wide open for us. We need to prioritize the presence of the Spirit, the proclamation of the gospel, and love for one another. We know these things will lead us closer to John 17 unity.

Dead Ends: Submit to our Authority

Having a common authority is a powerful form of natural unity. Complex human interaction is completely impossible without leadership hierarchies. Imagine a commercial airliner without a pilot, flight attendants, and a ground crew. Imagine a family without mom and dad. Imagine a nation without a government.

Human beings speak the language of authority and understand it implicitly. We constantly and effortlessly navigate a complex and overlapping system of authority structures that includes family, various levels of government, work, play, and religious structures.

Given the power and importance of spiritual and religious authority, it can be tempting for some to say "Let's all just agree on someone to follow," or worse, "Submit to our authority, or else!" While we can understand this impulse, this is not a way to build John 17 unity. It is wrong and it never works.

Instead, we learn from Jesus that the greatest (in authority) will be as a child and a servant of all. If you're looking around for the kind of authority Jesus wants us to submit to, look for the meek who are bearing the fruit of the Spirit and follow them.

Dead Ends: Compromising the Word of God

Another dead end is to compromise God's word in our pursuit of outward unity. It is very common for unity-minded movements to become so focused on the external act of bringing people together they forget that the unity they crave is only found in Jesus Christ, the Word. Real unity must agree with the written Word.

Scripture is clear, there are areas of conscience where disagreement and differing practices are permitted and even expected.[9] There are secondary issues where we can agree to disagree or learn from one another. However, there are also core issues where we must be in agreement. Is Jesus Christ just one way among many, along with Buddha and Mohammed, or is He the only way to the Father?

Is Christ the only begotten Son of God, or is He simply a man who led a good life?

Early in church history, it seemed that the identity of Christ was the most contentious issue. Recently in the west, issues of sexual identity have taken center stage.

Is it okay to "agree to disagree" on whether homosexual practice is a sin? Or, if a man can become a woman, and a woman become a man? While these matters of sexual immorality were settled in the Jerusalem

---

9   Romans 14, Colossians 2:16 Romans 14, Colossians 2:16-23, and many other passages speak to how we can handle secondary disagreements in love.

counsel in Acts 15, many have decided to tolerate evil in the name of unity. Thankfully, western Christians have the example of leaders in the global south standing up against these wicked practices and speaking truth to us. We will never have John 17 unity if we tolerate Jezebel.[10]

On the other hand, there are different styles of taking communion, different ways of baptizing people, different worship styles and practices, different points of teaching emphasis from Scripture. As St. Augustine is supposed to have said, "in essentials, unity; in non-essentials, liberty; in all things, charity." However, we must maintain unity in terms of the essentials of God's Word.

If we fail on this point, we are at risk of joining in an anti-Christ unity movement and coming under God's judgement. Remember, true unity is corporate holiness. The two cannot be separated.

Dead Ends: Lowest Common Denominator

Similar to compromising the essential truths of God's word for a false unity, is the dead end of "Lowest Common Denominator" unity. This involves bringing people together from a very broad spectrum and avoiding anything controversial. It seeks to establish unity on a very low, universally agreed upon basis. For instance, many political causes or social service movements, like a group of ministries serving the homeless, operate in this way.

There's nothing wrong with doing things like this. It's good for believers and unbelievers to do good works in their community. If your goal is to start a soup kitchen or promote a specific political issue, this can work. However, in terms of pursuing John 17 unity, the Lowest Common Denominator strategy will never work.

If you want to pursue John 17 unity, Christ Himself must be the common denominator, with His Word exalted and His Spirit in the

---

10 Revelation 2:20

midst. If we focus our attention on Him and put Him at the center while listening to and obeying His Word, we will soon find ourselves becoming one, as He and the Father are one.

Dead Ends: *Quid pro Quo*

Quid pro quo is Latin for "this for that." It speaks of arrangements where we trade value in order to get something else we want. These types of transactions are not bad in and of themselves. In fact, we use them most commonly when we purchase things with money. I pay three dollars and walk away with a cup of coffee. Everyone is happy.

While much of life operates on a *quid pro quo* basis, the Kingdom economy works differently. Jesus says, "Freely you have received, freely give." You've probably never been to a church that charges you to attend, even though the services offered are often of very high value. It is spiritually illegal to sell the goods of the Kingdom. They must be offered freely. You are welcome, but not required, to leave an offering.

In working for unity, one of the worst dead ends I've encountered is a *quid pro quo* attitude or mindset. I'll attend your prayer event if you attend my church event next month. I'll invite my network if you'll use your email list to sell my book. While *quid pro quo* dealings are routine and every day in the world, they are no basis for any type of unity effort. The Kingdom has a different type of economy.

Quid pro quo arrangements may temporarily bring more people together; however, they're not the people you want to build with if John 17 unity is your goal. Look for those with full hearts who want to freely give and freely receive.

Endgame: Will we be (Structurally) One?

It would be helpful as we pursue John 17 to have a clear idea of what the structural end-state will look like. Will these 45,000 denominations, or a large portion of them, somehow merge into a mega organization? Or will these structural separations remain while the power of the Spirit is at an all-time high and our hearts are knit together as one? Is it enough to be relationally one while maintaining structural divisions?

Perhaps the Spirit will bring us into a new type of organizational structure, one with the dynamism of the Spirit but the clearly defined leadership of the early church. I wish I knew our structural end-state. However, I must confess I cannot clearly see what God will do. I only know the Holy Spirit is the essential key to John 17 unity. Let's learn to follow Him, and we won't miss out.

On the other hand, we can decisively conclude that the enemy's counterfeit unity system (the new Babel) will absolutely be structural. Lacking the heavenly unity that comes from the Holy Spirit, structural and economic unity mechanisms will be essential and will be coupled with the ecstatic elements of demonic spiritual power, music, sexual immorality, and drugs—counterfeits for the joy of the Spirit and the power of our worship and love for one another.

I do not know if the church that experiences the fullness of John 17 will be structurally one. I do know that it will be full of the power and presence of the Holy Spirit and that we will experience love for one another at a level never seen before on earth. I know that the leadership will be humble, pure, and servant-hearted. The unbelieving world will confess the great magnitude of the Father's love for us.[11] I know that this united church will also experience persecution at levels not seen before in history.[12] We also know that corresponding to this great movement of unity will be a great falling away from the faith. And yet, those who persevere will experience love for one another at a level never seen before on earth.

---

11 John 17:23
12 Revelation 6:10-11, Matthew 24:21-22

Given the level of uncertainty that exists, we'd do well not to cling too tightly to our pre-conceived notions of what the answer to Jesus's prayer will look like. We have a very partial vision.

However, one thing is clear: We are seeking a union that only comes from the Holy Spirit. No one else can make us one as the Father and Son are one. Let's love and maintain the (structural) places in the church where God has placed us as we cry out to Him for the full union that is coming.

3

The Gift of Helps

In April of 2018, I was able to hear Rick Joyner speak in person for the first time. Rick is one of the fathers of the modern prophetic movement. As a younger believer who was growing in hearing God's voice, his weekly writings were influential and encouraging. After all these years, I was excited to be in the same room.

I was surprised by his calm, grandfatherly demeanor as he spoke to a room of about 300 people. His comments had all the warmth and familiarity of an intimate conversation over coffee as he wandered from topic to topic and insight to insight.

At one point, he shared a conversation he had with the Lord about John 17 unity.

"Lord, what's the most important spiritual gift for unity in the Body of Christ?"

The answer that came from the Holy Spirit surprised him: "The gift of helps."

The spiritual gift of helps is spoken of in 1 Corinthains 12:28:

> "And God has appointed in the Church first apostles, second prophets, third teachers, then miracles, then gifts of healings, helps, administrations, various kinds of tongues…"

Did you catch it in there? It's easy to miss, hidden in the middle of a list of eight gifts.

As Rick humorously shared, he thought the gift of helps had to do with making coffee for church on Sunday morning. To be honest, that was the extent of my understanding of helps as well.

Understanding the Gift of Helps

The actual gift of helps, thankfully, is much more than making coffee. It is a spiritual gift that enables the person who has it to assist others in completing their God-given assignments.

All of us have assignments from the Lord. These are specific roles and responsibilities that we must carry and complete. However, none of us can complete these God-given assignments alone. We all need help from others to accomplish what God has called us to do.

Let's think about it in the context of a family. As a father, I have a special role and assignment from God specific to my children. It would be inappropriate for me to shirk my responsibility, or for someone else to try and usurp my special role. It is mine.

However, as a father I regularly run into problems I can't solve. I need the help of other older men who serve as "father figures" for my children, especially their grandfathers. I also need the advice, counsel, and encouragement of other fathers. I desperately need the help of my wife if I am going to be adequate as a dad.

We could think of each divine assignment as belonging 80% to the person to whom it is given. However, the remaining 20% is something the person could never accomplish alone, no matter the level of gifting, grace, or natural talent. The gift of helps serves others by supplying what is lacking, by helping each part of the body complete their callings.

Chapter 3: The Gift of Helps

Galatians 6:2-5 is a clear example of how the gift of helps operates.

> "Bear one another's burdens and so fulfill the law of Christ. For if anyone thinks himself to be something when he is nothing, he deceives himself. But let each one examine his own work and then he will have rejoicing in himself alone and not in another. For each one shall bear his own load."

Paul's comments may be a bit confusing, but if we read the passage starting at the end, it becomes clear.

Each of us has our own load to bear, our own responsibilities, calling, and work to perform. We need to keep our eyes focused on that—are we bearing our load, or are we self-deceived?

However, to fulfill the law of Christ, to love one another as He has loved us, we need to help each other with our burdens. "Burdens" are the loads that are one person's responsibility but are too heavy for them to lift on their own. The gift of helps swoops in to help with these burdens.

The Woman

Once we notice it, the hidden gift of helps begins to appear everywhere throughout Scripture. First, we see it in Genesis 2:18:

> "It is not good for the man to be alone. I will make a helper[1] suitable for [comparable to] him."

Eve was the first person with the gift of helps, and immediately her gift led to unity.

> "Therefore, a man shall leave his father and mother and be joined to his wife and they shall become one flesh."
> Genesis 2:24, NKJV

---

[1] For those who like to study, the Hebrew word *ezer* for "help" or "helper" is a treasure trove.

Eve comes alongside Adam in a secondary but comparable role. It's easy to see that Adam would be unable to carry out his God-given assignment, to "be fruitful and multiply and fill the earth, and subdue it" apart from the help of Eve.

However, Adam was also unable to fulfill his priestly role of working and guarding the garden without Eve's help.[2]

In terms of the gift of helps, it is fair to say that women have an "unfair advantage" over men, since they possess it as part of God's creation gift to them.

Holy Spirit

One of the Holy Spirit's primary names is "the Helper."[3] We cannot follow God's commandments on our own. We need divine help. We cannot love one another as we ought. We need the Spirit. We cannot fulfill our God-given assignments and roles on our own. We need His help. We cannot pray as we should. The list goes on and on.

The Holy Spirit is the one who helps us in our weakness. And yet, His help does not absolve us of responsibility for our actions and decisions. We are responsible to walk in faith and express love for one another. We must stand in the midst of a hostile world—that is our part. And yet, we would never accomplish any of this apart from His help.

While it is true that the Holy Spirit helps us, in a deeper and more

---

2   Meredith Kline in *Kingdom Prologue*, and many others have noted how Adam's primary role in the garden was priestly. For instance, his mandate to "work it and guard it" uses the same Hebrew words that were given to the Levitical priests and their tabernacle ministry. This fascinating thread is beyond our current scope, but Eve was certainly a helper of Adam's primary calling as a priest in God's sanctuary of Eden.

3   John 14:16, 26. John 15:26, John 16:7.

ancient role, the Holy Spirit is the bond of union between the Father and the Son.

The Helper is the one who is constantly serving, constantly in motion back and forth between the Father and the Son conveying love, fullness, and glory! From before the foundation of the world, the help of the Holy Spirit has been the bond of perfect unity in God Himself. The Holy Spirit has always been the Helper and His help has always brought about perfect union.

Joseph the Cyprian

There is one New Testament believer who we clearly see operating in the gift of helps. Not surprisingly, he was one of the best-loved members of the early church. So much so that no one remembers his given name, Joseph the Cyprian.

We all know him by his nickname, Barnabas, "Son of Encouragement."

We first see Barnabas helping the Jerusalem church through a large financial gift in Acts 4. He is contrasted here with Ananias and Saphira, who are deceitful helpers, and end up being killed by the Holy Spirit. Giving financially is certainly part of the gift of helps.

However, we get a true sense of how Barnabas got his nickname in the story of the apostle Saul/Paul. After his conversion, the entire church in Jerusalem is afraid of Saul, and for good reason—he was just trying to arrest and murder them! However, Barnabas is the one who introduces him and vouches for him. Barnabas brings Saul into the fellowship of the apostles and leaders of the church. He sees something in Saul and helps unlock his apostolic gift.

Think about this: without Barnabas's help, there would be no Paul.

Later, in Acts 11, Barnabas is sent to investigate the Gentile believers in Antioch. At the time, it was a major shock for the Jewish disciples that non-Jews were following their national Messiah. There was a strong contingent in the early church urging these new converts to become circumcised and keep the ceremonial law of Moses. This was a make-or-break moment for the church. Thankfully, Barnabas, "a good man full of the Holy Spirit and faith," correctly identified what was happening in Antioch as the work of the Holy Spirit. He had the insight to discern that Gentiles did not need to become Jewish to follow Jesus.

The church in Antioch would serve as the greatest missional hub of the first century. No Barnabas, no Antioch.

Finally, Saul and Barnabas were the ones chosen by the Holy Spirit in Acts 13 as missionaries to carry the gospel throughout the Mediterranean region. It should be no surprise to us at this point that God would choose to pair someone with a strong gift of helps alongside the apostle Paul. This ministry partnership was a dynamic force multiplier.

No Barnabas, no Paul the missionary, no early church mission movement. The life of Barnabas is a clear example of how gift of helps works to strengthen, build, and unite the church.

Dead Ends: Don't Pick Up Someone Else's Load (The problem of over-helping)

Of course, everyone loves to be helped. And this leads us to the dark side of the gift of helps: taking on someone else's load. It is very common for those who have the gift of helps to take on too much for another person, preventing them from carrying the responsibilities and assignments that belong to them.

We see this often with mothers and children, where moms are sometimes hesitant to let children take appropriate risk and responsibility for their age. If the situation is not corrected, the coddled child will fail to develop resilience and other important life skills. The child will fail to mature.

Ministries see this all the time. People step in to assist someone else, enjoy the feeling of doing good, and then within a few months are overcommitted and burned out. Or those in the community with a bottomless well of need, people who are not walking in repentance, seek out and find the people with especially compassionate hearts. Such needy people who refuse to help themselves end up sucking the others dry, and no one is helped.

When helping moves into carrying someone else's proper load, the helper is being unjustly burdened. This is a very common pitfall and must be guarded against with discernment from the Spirit. We also need to make sure we are not being manipulated by guilt into doing something for others that they should rightly do for themselves. While these principles seem evident in theory, the practical application is often very messy. Discernment from the Spirit is needed at every step.

Keep in mind, the true gift of helps is about helping another person complete an assignment or role for God, helping someone do something they could never do for themselves. That's why you'll often find people who are making the most of their callings receiving the most help.

Dead Ends: Helping to Exalt Ourselves

The book of Acts juxtaposes the story of Ananias and Saphira to the introduction of Barnabas for a reason. Both Barnabas and Ananias and Saphira seem to be moving in a gift of helps. Both seem to be incredible blessings to the early church. However, Ananias and Saphira gave financially not to help others, but to make themselves look good. To make it even worse, they lied about their giving. Their deaths stand as a frightful warning against misusing the gift of helps for self-exaltation. Because the gift is so closely tied to the core identity of the Holy Spirit, we must be sure not to dishonor Him as we use it.[4]

We must guard against helping as a way of building ourselves up or exaggerating how much we are giving to others. Helps has a built-in humility and loves to work behind the scenes. It's not a pathway for selfish ambition or self-promotion.

How to Operate in the Gift of Helps

As I listened to Rick's message, I immediately recognized I had been operating in the gift of helps for years without knowing what it was. If you receive greater joy in helping others achieve success than in your own success, this is one sign you may have the gift of helps.

Here are some keys to operating in this gift.

See yourself as a servant to all.

"If you want to be great in God's Kingdom, learn to be the servant of all." Jesus understood the pathway to greatness was to serve everyone, and He lived as He spoke, giving His own life in service to each of us. If the Master lived this way, how much more so should we?

As you go about your day and encounter people, see yourself as someone who is there to help and serve them. If you find this attitude odd or foreign to you, spending time learning to serve through a helping role such as a waiter, nurse, parent of small children, janitor, or teacher may help you to cultivate a servant's attitude. If this seems too lowly or

---

4 Matt. 12:31 warns us that "blasphemy against the Spirit will not be forgiven." There seems to be a special protectiveness from Father and Son for the Spirit. Because helps is so tied to the Spirit's core identity, we should exercise special care not to be careless or misuse the gift. We don't want to end up like Ananias and Saphira.

beneath you, remember: if it was good enough for the Master, it is good enough for each of us.

Ask people "What are you concerned about?" and "Is there a way I could help?"

Often, when asked this question, people realize that they are the only one who can fully address their problem. The act of listening and expressing concern is a way of helping and serving. This is also a natural point where you can offer to pray for others. Prayer for others is often an initial expression of the gift of helps.

If they ask you for help, consider if you can do what they're asking—ask the Holy Spirit for help if you're not sure.

Consider if God is calling you to help the person in the way they're asking. You'll want to be generous but also consider the cost of following through and the danger of over-helping. This is where you'll need the Holy Spirit to provide discernment.

If you're not willing or available to help in the way they've asked, consider offering an alternative.

Explain that you're not able to do what they've asked but offer to serve them in another way they may not have considered. Oftentimes, this is where you both begin to understand one another and the gift of helps can begin to operate effectively.

In Conclusion

Like all of the gifts of the Spirit, every believer is able to operate in the gift of helps *to some extent* but some believers will operate in it as a primary gift. Almost all believers who have a primary calling to John 17 unity will move in the gift of helps.

This gift absolutely kills division. It is very hard to be envious or suspicious of people who are helping you from a pure heart. When someone helps us accomplish our assignments in God and serves us as a free gift, it's hard not to love them and be drawn into unity together.

The gift of helps is much more than making coffee on Sunday morning. It's a key part of the Father's plan to answer Jesus's prayer.

4

Divisions

"I know I'm called to unity. So why am I constantly in the middle of painful divisions?"

It was the summer of 2014, and I was having a miserable time following Jesus. We had moved to western Massachusetts in 2012, a move God had confirmed by prophetic words and numerous miraculous signs.

Nine months after moving to western Massachusetts, we had a painful split with some of our main ministry partners. We had anticipated serving together with them for the rest of our lives. We had prophetic promises from God together. How could this be happening?

Around this same time, we started a new house of prayer in our region. Our small team was faithfully praying twelve hours a week. After many months of faithful building and persevering through many difficulties, we began to experience an outpouring of the Holy Spirit in our community. Just as this breakthrough was happening, a spiritual mom and dad, a couple who had been influential in our decision to move to the region, attacked and disowned us. I was in complete shock. The pain was unreal, and it ultimately destroyed the small ministry our team had been laboring to build.

In this same season, I was strongly led by the Holy Spirit to pull together a collaborative partnership composed of several major Christian organizations to do something bigger together than any of them could do separately. Once again, God was speaking through many different people and confirming His leading with incredible signs. I was caught up in the whirlwind of excitement around what God was doing, simply honored to be a part of something so significant. Then, one of the major partners, a group I had introduced to the opportunity, decided to go after it on their own. I felt betrayed both by them and by the Lord: How could God lead me into a unity project that ended in division?

Finally, a close friend insisted on partnering with Christian groups championing sexual immorality in pursuit of unity. Scripture and plain reason convinced me this was not a "secondary issue" for followers of Jesus. After an extended process that left room for repentance, I was forced to separate. I felt like I had lost part of myself in the process.

Division is not Always Bad

It was during this season that I began to wrestle with a blind spot in my view of the world. God had called me to John 17 unity. However, the same Jesus that prayed "let them be one as we are one," and "peace, peace, I give to you" also said, "I did not come to bring peace, but a sword."

Is Jesus double-minded? Or could it somehow be that the Jesus who is praying for perfect unity is also the one who brings division? Could division now actually be a strategy for greater unity in the future?

The church currently has approximately 45,000 different denominations. Structurally, we are divided in thousands of pieces. Could this division, paradoxically, be part of God's master plan to answer Jesus's prayer in John 17?

God's Creative Power: Dividing for Greater Glory

As it turns out, this idea of bringing greater unity out of division comes right from the beginning of the Scriptures.

Starting in Genesis 1:3 with the creation of light, we see a division made between light and darkness, between day and night.

God continues to divide sky from seas, and sea from land. Each day of creation involves division and darkness. Each new day, He declares what He has made "good."[1] However, we are supposed to understand, each new day is better than the day before. The new divisions of each day produce a greater overall unity. Was the first day bad if the fifth day was good? No, day one was good, but day five is even better. God's creation moves from glory to glory. Division and darkness go before each new, more glorious day. Division and darkness are part of the path to greater unity of the whole.[2]

The Pattern Again: Death and Division Precede Glory and Resurrection

Moving on to the creation of the woman in Genesis 2, we see the same pattern.

God has declared everything He has made "good" up to this point, and so it is striking when He says it is "not good" for the man to be alone. As He moves to make a "helper fit for him," Adam is first subjected to futility,[3] naming the all the animals in his quest for his counterpart. When this fails, God places Adam into a deep, dark sleep, a death sleep.[4]

---

1   With the exception of the second day where He divides heaven from the waters, God declares each day to be good.

2   Acknowledgement here to James Jordan and the Theopolis institute. This treatment is deeply indebted to his excellent audio teachings on Genesis 1-3.

3   See Romans 8:20

4   *Tardema* used here is not the normal word for "sleep" in Hebrew. Often translated "deep sleep," "a sleep like death" is perhaps a better translation.

While Adam is in death sleep, God opens Adam's chest, removing a "side of Adam"[5] and uses this to create the woman. Adam is divided.

From the death and division of Adam, a new and greater unity comes forth: "For this cause, a man shall leave his father and mother and cleave to His wife, and the two shall become one flesh." Adam awakens from death sleep singing to his bride, "This is bone of my bone and flesh of my flesh…" He also emerges with a new name. Up to this point, he has been called "Adam," which comes from the Hebrew word "earth." Now, he is called Ish, another Hebrew word for man that sounds very much like Esh, the Hebrew word "fire."

In the sacrificial system of Moses, animals were divided in half before being "glorified" on the altar through fire, the resulting incense being a pleasing smell to God. In a way that parallels these sacrifices, Adam has also been divided and is now lit on fire, glorified in greater unity with his bride. The division of humanity into male and female has brought about a greater glory.

The second Adam, Jesus, underwent a similar division. Like Adam, He was placed in a deep sleep and His body was broken. When He awoke, He also beheld the second Eve,[6] who He is still bringing into complete unity. Now, we as His people are betrothed as His Bride in a New Covenant that has a much greater glory than the Old Covenant. Now, we ourselves are lit on fire by the indwelling Spirit as living sacrifices to God. However, all that we possess is due to the division of the Lord's body, which we celebrate every Sunday.

God's way of doing things in creation and through human history is to bring daylight after darkness, unity out of division, and resurrection

---

5   Once again, Adam's "rib" may be better translated as "side." There's a strong sense here that Adam is being divided.

6   Note that He is found by a woman, Mary, in John's gospel. All of the gospels have the second Adam discovered by women. This is no accident.

life out of death. As we have seen earlier, this pattern flows from the inner life of God. This pattern will continue through this age, although in age to come,[7] it will enter a new stage. Soon, there will be no more night, no more death, and no more division, nothing but uninterrupted enjoyment of His glory and revelry in His beauty.

Let's look at different types of division in Scripture used by God to bring about greater unity.

Types of Division that Lead to Unity

Pruning (John 15:2)

Spoken of in John 15, this division is performed by the Father Himself on fruitful parts of His body. While pruning is a positive thing and is meant to result in greater fruitfulness, it can be quite painful for the branch. It involves the loss of what in the past has been good and fruitful so that even more fruit can come forth. The Lord promises that all of His faithful followers will experience pruning.

Removal (John 15:2, 6 and Revelation 2-3)

In John 15, the Lord speaks of another group of followers who will be permanently cut off, thrown away, and burned in fire. As we learn in Revelation 2:5 when Jesus warns the church of Ephesus, this type of removal is possible not just for individuals but for entire city-wide churches.

This contributes to the unity of the entire Body by removing parts that are no longer bearing fruit. While this type of division may be a net-positive for the entire body, it should fill us with the fear of the

---

[7] Based on how this pattern flows from God's inner life that began before the foundation of the world, we might conclude it will continue forever and ever. However, the picture in Revelation 21-22 is one of no death, no division, and no darkness. Here again, we see the need to be led by Scripture rather than human reason even based on other parts of Scripture.

Lord. He is committed to the unity of His bride and will remove us if we do not agree with His leadership.

Excommunication (1 Corinthians 5)

In 1 Corinthians 5, Paul gives us a masterclass on handling believers who are unrepentant and living in gross sin. After time is given for repentance and they are still rebellious, they need to be removed from the fellowship. This is both for their own good, so they can recognize and repent of their sin, as well as for the good of the fellowship, so it is not divided and corrupted by approving or tolerating their sin.

Excommunication, while extreme, is a division that enables greater unity.

Division because of persecution (Acts 8:1, 11:19)

In the book of Acts, breakthroughs of the gospel into new territories often follow divisions of the body caused by persecution. For instance, in Acts 8 the body is scattered by persecution out of Jerusalem and into Judea and Samaria, leading immediately to many salvations and a fresh outpouring of the Holy Spirit with signs and wonders on the Samaritans.

In Acts 11:19, believers scattered by the persecution that began with Stephen land in Antioch, where the first predominantly Gentile church is established.

Just as God used the division of languages to drive humanity throughout the entire Earth, so God uses division caused by persecution to drive the spread of the gospel.

Division for mission (Acts 13)

During a time of worship and fasting in Acts 13, Paul and Barnabas are set apart (divided) by the Holy Spirit for a special mission.

Their division from their local fellowship in Antioch leads to one of the most famous and fruitful missionary partnerships of all time, but it was costly and painful for the brothers in Antioch to see Paul and Barnabas go. The Holy Spirit is the one who divides us for different purposes and functions, all to the benefit of the whole body.

Division among the brothers (Acts 15:39)

Just a few passages later, we have one of the saddest passages in the New Testament.

> "And there arose a sharp disagreement [between Paul and Barnabas] so that they separated from each other. Barnabas took Mark with him and sailed away to Cyprus…" Acts 15:39

Sometimes, even true believers will separate because of conflict and disagreement.

Excommunication sends someone "out" of the church preserving unity and holiness. Division among brothers represents division within the house. While we know it is not the will of God for this to happen, that doesn't mean that God won't use this in various ways.

Paul shares in 1 Cor. 11:18-19 that God uses factions in the church to reveal genuine and false disciples. God uses these types of painful divisions in our lives to form character, reveal personality flaws, and deepen our hunger and capacity for unity.

In this passage, the immediate consequence of the division is new leaders being raised up as missionaries and a multiplication of missions in the Mediterranean region. Even this painful division, the result of human sin and weakness, God used for the furtherance of the gospel. In a hopeful final footnote to this story, at the end of Pauls' life,[8] we hear him asking for Mark's help. Clearly, the breach that occurred years before had been mended.

---

8   2 Tim. 4:11

Death (1 Corinthians 15, 1 Thessalonians 4)

Death continues to divide the Body of Christ on earth. Many beloved brothers and sisters, faithful followers of Jesus, are no longer with us on earth. And yet, precious in the sight of the Lord is the death of His saints. The division caused by death is very painful but not permanent. At the return of the Lord, those who have fallen asleep in dishonor will awaken in honor, with incorruptible bodies like the body of our Lord Jesus. Death is not only our enemy, it is the enemy of our Lord and the final enemy that He will destroy.

Dead Ends: Becoming a Stumbling Block

While we should have confidence in the Father's ability to bring unity out of divisions, even divisions caused by human sin, we must do everything in our power not to be the cause of such divisions. As Jesus says, there are stumbling blocks that are necessary and are certainly coming. However, "woe to the one by whom the stumbling block comes."[9] Our duty is to live at peace with everyone, inasmuch as it depends on us. While it may be true that where sin abounds, grace abounds all the more, it is also very false to also conclude, "let's sin so that more good may come." Remember, while God may be using divisions to bring about the ultimate unity of His people, He is able to do that with or without you. We don't want to end up among the cut-off branches that Jesus describes in John 15. We don't want to be the cause of unnecessary division.

Moves of the Spirit Often Cause Division

From the vibrant chaos of the first century church, by the second century the church had a well-defined structural unity with bishops

---

9 Matthew 18:7

over city-wide churches, and many local churches meeting under the city bishop, and these leaders in relationship and correspondence with one another.[10]

Today, the church is in a new, structural chaos, with thousands of different denominations.

Many of these divisions came about because of human sin, but many others occurred because God was doing something new and different. Whenever there is a fresh outpouring of the Spirit, we see new divisions come forth. Often, these newer movements are some of the most vital and most productive parts of the church. The very life of the early church that so inspires us was born out of a division from existing Judaism, a division that was incredibly painful for the Lord and the apostolic generation. Church history has seen that pattern play out over and over again, as leaders in established church movements persecute and resist the new thing God is doing.

Think of the new treasures that have emerged from church divisions, from the Protestant Reformation to the various waves of the modern Pentecostal movement. Just as new treasures have been discovered, old treasures have also been preserved because of division. The Eastern Orthodox church to this day preserves almost unchanged a form of worship developed in the first four centuries. The diversity of forms of worship, gifts of the Spirit, manifestations of the Spirit, operations of the Spirit—all of these diverse expressions are able to flourish in the modern church because of our divisions. Let's remember, the Spirit is the uniter, but He is the seven-fold Spirit of God.[11] In Acts 2:3, He appears as "divided tongues of fire resting on each one of them."

---

10 Taking this description from the letters of St. Ignatius of Antioch. See *Eary Christian Fathers* compiled by Cyril Richardson to gain a fuller picture of the Church from 100-300 A.D.

11 Isaiah 11, Revelation 1:4

Holy Spirit is the person in the Trinity who is multiple, diverse, and constantly in motion. His wisdom is "manifold," or many-sided. Because the Spirit is uniquely multi-faceted, He is able to make we who are many, one.

Trust the Plan Accounts for our Failings

God is moving through our divisions, those caused by sin, and those brought about by the Holy Spirit, to prepare us individually and corporately for a higher and deeper unity. All He has to do is say the word and send fire on the altar, and our current state of external division will be glorified into a heavenly unity the likes of which the world has never seen.

Amid these external divisions, we can trust our Father to bring a mature unity in answer Jesus's prayer: Let them be one as we are one. In fact, somehow the existence of such great divisions fills me with even greater hope and joy.

From the beginning of creation and through the whole story of redemption, our God brings greater glory and greater unity out of death, darkness, and division.

5

"Meditate on My Love For You"

It was evening, August 19, 2009, and I was exhausted, trying to fall asleep.

I had spent the day in conflict. A friend of mine was in obvious sin, and when confronted, refused to repent.

Having banged my head against a wall all afternoon, my heart was sensitive to the power of self-deception blinding my friend. Sin lies to us and makes us lie to ourselves, trapping us in the dark.

As I shared my frustrations with the Lord in prayer, I was reminded that just a few weeks earlier, I had been the blind one. I had seriously wronged an older brother in the Lord while thinking I was in the right. Thankfully, after several months, the Holy Spirit spoke to me, corrected me, and I apologized to my brother.

And yet, I trembled to think about the damage I caused. In my zeal to do justice, I had committed injustice. In trying to do the right thing, I had made matters worse, causing real harm to my brother and even his whole family.

It was clear to me I was not someone to be trusted.

The Likeness of the Father

As I tried to sleep that night, I found God was speaking to me. I needed to make myself available to Him. Gently stepping away so as not to wake my pregnant wife, I retreated to my home office to listen to the Lord.

Witnessing these failures in my friend and in myself had created a cry in my heart: "Lord, I want to be someone you can trust…and someone I can trust." My heart was crying out to God for true righteousness, for an end to come of having to second-guess every impulse of my heart.

I was filled with an intense longing for righteousness, the genuine hunger and thirst to be "right on the inside." How much longer would I have to contend with the traitor within—my own sin?

My desire for righteousness continued to grow and grow, as tears quietly flowed. Soon, I was having a conversation with God that I recorded in my journal.

He asked me, "What do you want?"

Somehow, I knew this was a Solomon-type moment. Just as God gave Solomon a chance to ask Him for anything, now He was giving me the same opportunity. I knew in this holy moment I'd receive whatever I requested. Briefly, a worried thought flashed through my mind. What if I ask for the wrong thing? What if I blow it? But somehow, a response presented itself to me.

"I want your likeness, Father. I want to look just like you, to be just like you. I want to be just like Jesus Your perfect Son."

The Lord responded: "That is a good prayer and one I am willing to answer."

But I had more questions for Him: "Lord, what should I do to move in this direction?"

"Meditate on my love for you," came the unexpected response.

As He said these words, immediately I saw myself sitting at a piano, singing about God's love in our local prayer room. I knew my times of prayer would forever be different from that day forward.

He continued, "Once you know how much you are loved by me, everything else will flow from this."

"Is there anything else I can do to attain it?"

He gently corrected me, "Do not attain it; receive it as a gift."

Transforming the Place of Prayer

God continued to speak to me that night about many other things, including a significant ministry assignment I would walk out over the next two years.

However, the phrase, "Meditate on my love for you," and its connection to righteousness and the likeness of the Father, would fundamentally transform my personal life and my prayer life from that day forward.

Here are some of the changes that took place immediately in the aftermath of this word.

From Revival to the Love of God

I know it can sound selfish to "meditate on God's love for you." However, I'm convinced there's nothing more unselfish that we can do. Until we receive and understand the Father's love for us, we will never be able to love others with that same love. As the Scripture says, "We love because He first loved us." As I meditated on the love of God, I became more established in His love, and got better at releasing that love to others.

In this season, prayer shifted from a focus on petitions and requests to meditating on His nature and character.

Prayer was no longer mostly about problems for God to fix, injustice to be remedied, or even revival. It became a regular encounter with my Father, who also happened to be the Creator of the universe. Because He was so much greater, it made sense to praise Him, to listen, and to receive from His bounty.

Yet somehow, there seemed to be more answered prayer than ever before.

I Discovered How Biblical it was to Meditate on God's Love

One of the greatest scandals of the New Covenant is that the divine love of God the Father for God the Son is now being shared with human beings. This mystery is hidden in plain sight in the Scripture, but we can't actually see it unless Holy Spirit opens our eyes.

John 17:26 says,

> "I [Jesus] made Your [the Father's] name made known to them, and I will continue to make it known, *so that the love with which you have loved me may be in them*, and I in them."

John 15:9 says,

> "As the Father has loved me [Jesus] *so have I loved you. Abide in my love.*"

In Ephesians 3:14-21, Paul asks God for a full revelation of Christ's love so that "you may be filled *to all the fullness of God.*"

I quickly learned that the Lord was really calling me to have prayer times where I learned to abide in Him and in His love. By making this my focus in the place of prayer, I was allowing the love of God that was mine as a child of God to flow into my spirit and transform my thinking, correcting wrong thought patterns that I had picked up from the world. I was living out the reality of being a branch of Jesus, allowing His love to circulate through me like sap in a grapevine.

God's Presence Increased, along with Trials

When I think about this season, there are three things I remember: fear and agony from financial trials, combined with crippling uncertainty about what I was doing in ministry, and powerful encounters with the love of God that made me forget about the pain and keep moving forward. Some days I felt bi-polar. In prayer, God's presence was exploding with light and love. It was joy unspeakable and full of glory! In ministry, I was bearing fruit and seeing God's favor in incredible new ways. But the pressure was unbearable. Only revelation of the love of God kept me from quitting.

The Love of God Became the Biggest Thing in my Life

I wish I could say that I'm fully walking in the likeness of the Father. That I can trust myself completely to be righteous as I prayed on that night. That would be a lie—I still struggle with the traitor within.

However, I can say this: the love of God has become the biggest thing in my life. Spending long seasons of time receiving His love, often through singing songs to Him about His love for me and His nature has transformed me.

I may still be living in the desert of this age, but now there is a deep, pure, cool well of water where I live. I may not always be drinking, but I always know where to find my next drink. Even when I forget His love for a moment, I can always return, remember, and refresh my soul in His love that surpasses knowledge.

How Being Loved by God Fuels John 17 Unity

The community of perfect unity described in John 17 is made up of people who know the Father has loved them just as He loved Jesus. Their knowledge and awareness of the Father's love reaches such a level that not only are they personally and corporately aware of receiving the Father's love in this way (John 17:26), but unbelievers can see it and are forced to confess that "you [Father] have loved them [the disciples] as You have loved Me [Jesus]" (John 17:23).

We ought to meditate on the Father's love for us until it spills and overflows into every aspect of our lives. As the church truly and deeply begins to perceive this reality from the Father and then reflect it to one another, we will see the "perfect unity" of John 17 begin to manifest.

There is nothing more significant we can do than grow in revelation of God's love for us.

Dead Ends: God's Love is not His Only Character Trait

It's hard to find any downside to meditating on the love of God. In reality, there is no "downside." However, there are several pitfalls to avoid as the love of the Father grows larger in our eyes.

It's important to remember that the God of love we are encountering through Christ is a thoroughly beautiful, complex, and terrifying Person. The God who loves us like Jesus and desires for all to come to know His love is also the God who flooded the whole Earth and rained fire and brimstone on Sodom and Gomorrah. He is the God who will perfectly punish all sin.

He is compassionate towards sinners, but His compassion and kindness are unto repentance—if repentance does not come, judgment will eventually follow.

There's a temptation when we experience revelation of the love of God to forget about His justice and His wrath or to minimize these parts of His nature.

Yes, He is the kindest, most compassionate person we will ever meet. And yes, Hell and the final judgement are still necessary. Let's not fall into the trap of thinking we can be more compassionate than God or of oversimplifying His nature.

Dead Ends: God's Love will not Protect You From Hardship

The season when I first began to deeply encounter the love of God was one of the most difficult periods of my life.

In the place of prayer, I was captivated and overwhelmed by encounters with the love of God.

My day-to-day experience was completely different. I was constantly being crushed by trials and tribulations. When I look back at the details of what happened during that season, I wonder, "How did I make it?" In the moment I wondered, "How could the God who loves me so much allow me to suffer so much?"

And then I would experience His love again, forget all about my problems, and the cycle would repeat.

God loves us as He loved Jesus, who is called "a man of sorrows, and acquainted with grief." The love of God is meant to empower you to move through sorrow and trial, not to protect you from them.

"In this world, you will have trouble." It's a promise—you will have trouble. "But fear not, I have overcome the world."[1]

Dead Ends: Don't Become a Stagnant Pool

In the state of Minnesota, the land of a thousand lakes, they like to joke that the state bird is the mosquito.

I got to experience this firsthand one summer while canoeing in the

---

1 John 16

boundary waters between the United States and Canada. One night, I picked out a campsite next to a waterfall with fast-flowing water. I figured the moving water would prevent the mosquitoes from breeding. Surprisingly, the insects were worse at that campsite than at any other spot on our trip.

Curious, I walked to the large, low waterfall and took a closer look.

The torrents of running water concealed a secret: all along the rocks that formed the waterfall were hundreds of shallow, still pools of water—perfect breeding grounds for mosquitoes.

The torrent of God's love is meant to flow into us in order to flow out to others. If we are only receivers and stop releasing the love of God, we become stagnant pools and attractive to the demonic. If we allow the love of God to flow into us and then out to others, the life of God continues to flow and there is nowhere for the enemy to land. Releasing what God has poured into you opens space in your heart for Him to give you more and multiplies the effect of the love of God.

Stay in the flow: don't become a stagnant pool beside the torrent of the love of God.

As the apostolic poet says, "Beloved, let us love one another. For love is of God, and anyone who loves has been born of God and knows God. He that does not love does not know God, for God is love." 1 John 4:7-8

If we receive the love of God without sharing it with one another, we testify that we have not received the love of God in reality.

The Goal: Love One Another as I Have Loved You

In most team sports like football, baseball, basketball, and soccer, the ball is the main focus. Coaches tell their players all the time: "Keep your eye on the ball."

The love of the Father for the Son is the ball. The Father threw it to the Son, the Son threw it back to the Father. They were playing catch with it before the foundation of the world.

Now, somehow they have thrown the ball to us. And they want us to do the same thing here on earth.

Why are the Father and Jesus pouring their love into us, in the same way they love one another? It's so that we will love one another as Jesus has loved us.

    The love of the Father
        for the Only Begotten Son
            has become
        the love of Father God
    for all His children.

    The love of Jesus
        for His brothers
            has become
        the love we give
    to one another.

    The love of God
        for God
            has become
        the love of God
    for His people.

    The love of God
        for His people
            has become
        our love
    for one another.

        The love of Heaven
            has descended
                now we throw it
                    back and forth
                      on earth.

JESUS GETS WHAT HE PRAYS FOR

The church that Jesus died for is destined to get better and better at this divine game of catch until it is truly said, "Look how God loves them—they are truly one, just as the Father and Son are one."

6

Choose the Lower Seat

"I wonder if we can get seats at the table right next to him?"

It was evening, and my friend and I were busy turning a church worship space into a banquet room. As young men in our twenties, zealous for the Lord, we were excited at the possibility of rubbing shoulders with one of the famous speakers who was sitting at the head table. We were discussing how to best position ourselves to be able to interact with him.

My eyes were drawn to the other side of the room. "What if we took Jesus literally? Why don't we take the lowest seat we can find in the entire room?" As I shared these words, both my friend and I felt the presence of God.

That night, we picked out the farthest seats we could find from the main speaker. We were among the last to go through the food line. However, as the meal progressed and we interacted with our tablemates, we were surprised to learn they were close relatives of the guest of honor. After he had finished eating, the main speaker quickly headed over to our table, bypassing all the others, and pulled up a chair next to us.

My friend was unable to speak—I could see he was having an encounter with the Holy Spirit. I could hardly keep my laughter bottled up. Jesus's counsel was not just true in some abstract, spiritual sense. It was utterly practical. Taking the best seat would not have worked. But taking the lowest seat works every time.[1]

Greatness in the Kingdom of God

> "Jesus called them together and said, 'You know that the rulers of the Gentiles lord it over them, and their high officials exercise authority over them. Not so with you. Instead, whoever wants to become great among you must be your servant, and whoever wants to be first must be your slave— just as the Son of Man did not come to be served, but to serve, and to give his life as a ransom for many.'" Matthew 20:25-28, NIV

In Matthew 20:25-28, Jesus contrasts the greatness of the "rulers of the Gentiles" who "lord it over" those beneath them. Their great ones "exercise authority over them." In contrast, among Jesus's followers, "whoever would be great among you must be a servant and whoever would be first must be a slave." Jesus Himself provides the blueprint for a new definition of greatness: "just as the Son of Man came not to be served but to serve and to give his life as a ransom for many."

Jesus's teaching on true greatness comes in the middle of a dispute among His disciples about who would be the greatest.

Notably, He doesn't tell them to stop desiring to be great, to be first, or to be the best. Everyone who has children knows that they all want to be the greatest ballplayer and the strongest hero. Telling your children, "Stop wanting to be great," would deny the deepest desires of their heart. The desire to pursue greatness is hardwired into us. It's part of the image of God.

---

1   Luke 14:8-11

Instead of changing their goal, Jesus shows them that their image of greatness is weak and foolish.

They are after a cheap, imitation greatness—a knock-off of the genuine article. They're chasing the same thing ignorant Gentiles are chasing, people who don't know the true God, people who are like foolish children fighting over a toy.

Real greatness is modeled on God's greatness. He is the greatest of all—so true greatness must be modeled on His inner life. And Jesus has come to break open God's enormous heart and reveal the greatness of God once and for all.

In heaven, where there is no lack, it is greater to give than to receive. The more you give, the greater you are. Father God is the greatest, the one who gives all to all.

From eternity past, the Father gives Himself completely to the Son. He gives His fullness to the Son. The greatness of the Father is also the Father's humility. Similarly, the Son fully gives Himself to the Father. He lays down His life in obedience and imitation of the Father.

The Father and the Son then give themselves to the world. This is true, kingly greatness, the greatness of the Sun that constantly shines on the righteous and the wicked, giving gifts freely to all. The greatness of God is also the humility of God.

Jesus says, "Come to me, all who labor and are heavy laden, and I will give you rest. Take my yoke upon you, and learn from me, for I am gentle and lowly in heart, and you will find rest for your souls. For my yoke is easy, and my burden is light." Matt. 11:28-30

How could it be that the God who created all things, the great and majestic one, whose presence is shrouded in unapproachable burning, is also gentle and lowly to the core? It is because His greatness is expressed most fully in His complete and utter generosity. The greatest is the one who gives all and serves all.

Much has been made about the need for "servant-leadership" based on this saying of Jesus. We could define servant-leadership as leading in a way that primarily benefits those being led rather than the person at the top. It includes having the attitude of a servant as opposed to being a "gentile" leader looking for money, fame, and status and using others as a means to our own goals. This is certainly true: we need leaders like this. If we are called into leadership, we must model our actions on Jesus's words.

However, this passage is not primarily about leadership. It applies equally to the janitor as to the chairman of the board. He is not evaluating us based on our position in a leadership hierarchy, He is evaluating us on how we live as a servant of all, whether we are throwing out the trash or presenting to the board.

The pathway to true greatness is to be a servant and a slave to others—to exchange our lives for their lives. This is what it means to be king—to become the servant of all. And the beauty of it is we can do this no matter what our role is. God enjoys a janitor who is a servant to all more than a grasping CEO. And he enjoys a CEO who is a servant to all more than a resentful janitor.

This is true because this is the way God is. And Jesus acted out the inner life of God for us in real time. He showed us what it means to truly be a king.

God with a Towel

John 17 unity begins with John 13 humility.[2]

Jesus, rising from His seat at the head of the table, removes His glorious outer garment and replaces it with a towel, wrapping it around

---

2   John 13:1-17 was also discussed at length in Part 2.2

His waist. He pours water into a basin and washes His disciples' feet. The one through whom all things were created washes the feet of His creatures. He washes the feet of His weak friends, men who in a few hours will abandon and deny Him. He even washes Judas, His betrayer.

After, He removes the towel, puts on His outer garments, and returns to His place at the head of the table.

He asks a question: "Do you know what I have done for you?"

He has given them an example. He is their Lord and Master. He is much greater than them, and yet He served them in the humblest way imaginable. The conclusion is that they, who are much lower than Jesus, ought to serve one another in the same way.

He ends by promising a blessing for all who would follow His example, "Now that you know these things, you will be blessed if you do them." John 13:17, NIV

The generation that will see John 17:23 fulfilled will walk in the blessing of John 13:17.

Embody Humility

"If you know these things, you will be blessed if you do them."

One clear takeaway from John 13 and Matthew 20 is that humility is not only an attitude of our hearts. It is something we must act out and embody. The blessing of John 13:17 does not come to those who merely know they should serve others in lowest humility. It comes from doing it.

We will be in situations where we must choose where to sit, both literally and figuratively. We can choose to take the lowest seat. We can also choose to wash the feet of those Christ died for—in fact, we have opportunities to do this daily.

Early in my ministry I heard the Spirit say to me, "Die every chance you get." I believe the Lord was clearly instructing me on how to be great. I would have regular opportunities to die. By saying yes to those opportunities, I would make progress in the Kingdom. Serving Jesus often feels like one death after another.

Good. That is a sign we are choosing the way of wisdom.

Becoming a Kingdom Entrepreneur

As we begin to act out what Jesus has told us, learning to become a servant to all, Jesus's way of doing things will stop being weird and begin to make intuitive sense. We will begin to see all kinds of incredible investment opportunities, ways that we can increase our wealth, our greatness, our "status" and honor in the Kingdom.

Because the world does not have eyes to see what creates true wealth, wealth that lasts forever, Kingdom investments can often be had at extremely low cost.

As He instructs us on how to be Kingdom entrepreneurs, Jesus teaches us a new way to throw a party.[3]

Using Kingdom eyes, it's obvious that throwing a party for your rich friends is not a good investment. They already have food, and if you throw one for them, they'll likely throw a party for you. You'll be rewarded when they repay you. Nothing is given to them, and thus nothing is gained. That stock has already peaked—don't buy it.

In contrast, if you throw a party for those who are poor and hungry, now you're making money in the Kingdom. They can't pay you back, so God will reward you and make a deposit in your heavenly bank account. Now, you're learning to invest. You're learning how to make money in the Kingdom.

As you put humility into action, strangely, no one will be jealous of you for doing it—everyone will just be thankful. When we act out

---

3   Luke 14:12-14

the inner life of God on earth, it creates surprising love reactions from those around us. You are obtaining true riches, but doing so creates no resentment.

It's possible to go too far with this "crass" type of reasoning. However, we also need to make sure we go as far as Jesus goes. He is the one who told us we had a heavenly bank account and that we should be more concerned about what treasures we had stored in that account than in our J.P. Morgan Chase investment account.[4]

When you see something important falling through the cracks and no one is taking responsibility, that is a "buy low" opportunity. God may be opening a door for fruitful ministry and investment. At the end of the day, the greatest investment is always going to be in people. People will live forever. Your actions in this life to bless and care for others are a heavenly investment that will continue accruing value for all of eternity.

Caring for orphans, widows, and the poor is always a good place to start. James calls this "true religion" (James 1:27). However, opportunities to serve in the grace of God are boundless. Look for neglected areas with a large growth potential. In my life, I've continually found "buy low" opportunities in the areas of prayer and unity. There are usually no salaries for those who work between organizations, uniting believers, or those who are stirring up prayer. And yet, that work is critical to what God is doing in the earth and the return on investment is potentially massive. May God open our eyes to see the opportunities for eternal wealth all around us. May we all grow incredibly great and rich in God's eternal Kingdom.

Dead Ends: False Humility

In contrast to the joy and glory of real humility, false humility is hideous and repulsive.

---

[4] Jesus's concept of "treasure in heaven."

If real humility is a steak dinner, false humility is a rotting remnant of the same meal a week later in the compost heap on a hot summer's day. In American politics, false humility is an epidemic. Many have voted for a man who was unapologetically arrogant precisely because it was preferable to false humility.

I think in the final analysis, arrogance is most likely preferable to false humility. At least with arrogance you are getting the truth. False humility is lipstick on a pig.

False humility will come with a lot of religious-sounding language, self-deprecation, and putting yourself down. People who are genuinely humble know who they are, know their value to God, their position, and their assignment. They serve like kings and queens of the most high God. They look like Jesus. Self-possessed, wise and strong, yet with a gentle, lowly heart.

False humility is an ugly imitation. At all costs, avoid it.

Dead Ends: No Leadership

Another dead end is the idea that the very existence of leadership *at all* is what is driving pride. If we could do away with leadership, we would all be humble.

This idea is far from biblical. While there is certainly an equality that we all share before God, we all have different roles and functions in the Body of Christ and this includes leadership roles. Even within the Godhead, the Father is the leader of the Son and the Spirit, and yet there is perfect, self-giving humility.

Removing leadership functions in the family, the church, or any organization will foster chaos, not humility, and it does nothing to eliminate pride and envy from our hearts. Instead, we need humility applied to each role, relationship, and function.

We cannot get away from the problem of human pride with a perfectly flat organizational structure. It's chaos and it doesn't work—don't try it.[5]

Dead Ends: Weakness instead of Meekness

A strong and arrogant person, a great man of the Gentiles, might mistake a meek man for a weak man. This is understandable since the two are pursuing greatness along different lines. One is seeking earthly wealth, power, influence. The other is seeking heavenly wealth, authority, and influence. One is minding the things of earth, the other is thinking about God's things.

As we are learning meekness, given its contrast to worldly strength, we may be tempted to just "do the opposite" of what the world does. If the world pursues money, I will be poor. If the world craves influence, I will become as uninfluential as possible. If the world craves strength, I will become weak.

This is another dead end. God's way of greatness is not simply the opposite of the world's way. It's doing things heaven's way. God wants us to prioritize heavenly wealth, spiritual strength, and heavenly influence depending on the grace of God, following His voice, living by faith. He does not want us to stop pursuing glory. He wants us to pursue the glory that comes from God, not what comes from men.

Heavenly humility says in Romans 12:3:

> "...by the grace given to me I say to everyone among you not to think of himself more highly than he ought to think, but to think with sober judgement, each according to the measure of faith that God has assigned."

---

[5] I'm speaking here largely out of my own person experience of trying to do this, but I have also seen many others try and fail. While some leadership structures are better for certain applications, we will always need leadership.

Our pathway forward in humility is thinking of ourselves rightly according to the grace and faith God has given us. This does not mean being weak and having no backbone.

We must be careful not to be overly deferential to others and allow the enemy room to come in with false teaching and false ideas. While deferring and honoring one another is an important aspect of humility, there will be regular moments where humility looks like standing up for truth in the face of opposition, or using your leadership authority to protect others from predators, false teachers, and deceivers.

The same Jesus who was gentle and lowly of heart was also the one who stood against the lies of the Pharisees, pronounced woes, and cleansed the temple with a whip.

As in all things, our Lord bears the likeness of the Father. We can't just react against poor leadership models we have seen. We must walk as He walked, think as He thought, reason as He reasoned, and live as He lived.

The Coming Glory of Humility

John 17 unity is only possible through John 13:17 humility.

The Great Commission in Matthew 28:20 is only possible through the true greatness of Matthew 20:28.

The generation that sees John 17 fulfilled will model the greatness of the Kingdom expressed in humility and service to one another. We could even say the fullness of the blessing promised in John 13:17 is the fullness of unity prayed for in John 17. The generation that fulfills the Great Commission will have to walk in true greatness.

As more and more people, and especially those called to lead the church, learn to walk as Jesus taught us, it will lead to a new normal. Why would we fight one another for status, money, or fame when our glory is found in giving those things up for each other?

As the way of Jesus begins to go viral, and repentance touches leadership in deep places, a genuine, Christ-like humility will begin to be the new normal for His people. Everyone will be more eager to serve than to be served. Everyone will be honoring others above themselves. This virtuous cycle, like the inner life of the Father and Son, will begin to release grace upon grace upon grace. I cannot wait to be part of this community of Kingdom greatness, and I'm giving everything I have now with this as my goal.

The amazing thing about Kingdom culture is it creates no jealousy.

When my brother honors me above himself, I know he is greater in the Kingdom than me. But I'm not jealous because I can see he loves me, and his greatness is blessing my life. His greatness is for me—it's part of me, and I want him to be great! We come alive in a community of meekness in submission to the Holy Spirit.

Jesus is meek and humble at heart. He learned it from His Father. And now, we're learning it from our Teacher, Holy Spirit. And if we keep studying with our divine Tutor, we're going to wake up one day in a community of humility where we are "perfectly one."

7

Lay Down Your Life

Several years ago, I was sitting with a group of about thirty other Christian leaders. The participants were gifted and skilled, people of influence who also walked in humility. There was a real spirit of encouragement as each one shared in turn with the others what they were working on.

As I sat in this room, surrounded by these amazing people, the Lord began to speak to me.

"I'm glad that you're 'for' one another."

Right away, I knew what the Lord meant. He was drawing a contrast between being in competition and being "for" each other. Those of us in the room were all in a place of rejoicing in each other's successes and cheering each other on, as opposed to being in competition or envious. It was clear this group of people was on the right track.

"Now, I want you to be 'for' one another."

In my mind's eye, I saw bread and wine.

Immediately, I knew what the Lord was saying.

It's not enough not to be at each other's throats or even rejoicing in each other's success.

For John 17 unity to fully manifest, I must lay down my life for you, just as Christ laid down His life for me. Just as His body was given for us, He is calling us to give our lives for one another.

"This is my body given for you."

This is what John 17 unity looks like. Voluntarily giving up your life so others can live.

Two Kinds of Life

In the gospel of John, there are two words translated as "life" in English that are used very differently.

One is the Greek word *zoe*.

Every time Jesus speaks about "eternal life," He uses the word *zoe*. *Zoe* is a spiritual type of life that is essential to Jesus's mission. This is the life He is offering to everyone who believes. In fact, He even claims to be "the *Zoe*." As students of God's inner life, you can probably guess that the kind of life Father and Son exchange eternally is *zoe*-life. Having "eternal *zoe*-life" is to possess life as God possesses it, forever and ever and in overflowing abundance. If you have *zoe*-life, there is a gushing fountain inside of you that will never run dry. The indwelling Holy Spirit is the only source of *zoe*.

The other Greek word translated as life is *psyche*. You're probably familiar with words like "psychology," which are built on this Greek word. *Psyche* is used ten times in the Gospel of John, eight of those times by Jesus.

Psyche-life is different from *zoe*-life. It's the life of the soul, the union of your mind and your body here on this earth. Your *psyche*-life is you. It's your body, your inner life, your desires, your mind, and by extension would include your possessions, your reputation, your influence, and abilities.

Whenever Jesus talks about *zoe*-life He is speaking about God's inner life, the eternal, abundant life He wants to share with us.

Whenever Jesus talks about *psyche*-life, He talks about death.

Zoe and *Psyche* in Contrast

John 12:20-28 clarifies the distinction between *zoe* and *psyche* by using them side-by-side.

> "Now there were some Greeks among those who went up to worship at the festival. They came to Philip, who was from Bethsaida in Galilee, with a request. 'Sir,' they said, 'we would like to see Jesus.' Philip went to tell Andrew; Andrew and Philip in turn told Jesus."
>
> "Jesus replied, 'The hour has come for the Son of Man to be glorified. Very truly I tell you, unless a kernel of wheat falls to the ground and dies, it remains only a single seed. But if it dies, it produces many seeds. **Anyone who loves their (*psyche*) life will lose it, while anyone who hates their (*psyche*) life in this world will keep it for eternal (*zoe*) life.** Whoever serves me must follow me; and where I am, my servant also will be. My Father will honor the one who serves me.'"
>
> "'Now my (*psyche*) soul is troubled, and what shall I say? "Father, save me from this hour"? No, it was for this very reason I came to this hour. Father, glorify your name!'"
> John 12:20-28, NIV

As the first non-Jews in the entire gospel approach Him, Jesus knows it is time.[1] The one who has said, "My hour has not come" for the first eleven chapters[2] now says, "The hour has come for Son of Man to be glorified."

---

1 The nations coming "ripe," evidenced by the Greeks asking to see Jesus, is a sign to Jesus that the hour of His death has come.

2 Jesus and the gospel author have repeatedly stated "my hour has not yet come" throughout Chapters 1-11, beginning in John 2. Thus, when Jesus says "the hour has come..." it is highly significant.

It is time. The moment He has been waiting for has arrived. The nations are ripe for the harvest. It's time to reunite them back to God. But the cost of reuniting scattered humanity is unfathomable.

Jesus is going to voluntarily lay down His *psyche*-life, planting his *psyche*-life in the ground so it can be multiplied and bear fruit. He knows that He is only laying down His *psyche*-life for a time. He will pick it up again after He lays it down. Despite knowing this, His *psyche* (soul) is troubled, knowing the pain, dishonor, and death that are His portion. And yet, Jesus knows this is the reason He came into the world.

Finished Work and Model for Life

We see clearly that Jesus is speaking of His coming death on the cross, the finished work that opens the door to Paradise for all of us. Jesus giving up His *psyche*-life is a unique act in world history. He is the only-begotten Son of God. No one else could ever die to save the nations from sin and reunite them under the Creator.

Because of the unique power of what He is about to do, it is notable that His emphasis is not on the uniqueness of His sacrifice, but on the requirement for His students to die in the same way.

He is giving us a pattern to follow and imitate. He is showing us what we must do to live. Anyone who loves their *psyche*-life will lose it. Everyone who hates their *psyche*-life in this world will keep it for eternal *zoe*-life.

> "Whoever serves me must follow me; and where I am, my servant also will be."

In other words, I am going to the cross to lay down my *psyche*-life for you. Why don't we meet there?

Sometimes, believers mistakenly think because Jesus laid down His life for us, we don't have to lay down our lives. His work is finished.

There is nothing more for us to do.

This is certainly true in terms of our personal salvation. We can't add anything to what Christ has done for us. The work is finished and perfect. We can never be saved by our works—it's by the free gift of God!

However, as Jesus clearly says, our *psyche*-life must be laid down. The cross is not only our salvation, it is our pattern of life.

While we are not saved *by* works, we are saved *for* works.[3] Jesus has saved us so we can lay down our lives with Him. Those who love their *psyche*-life eventually lose it anyway. Those who hate their *psyche*-life paradoxically transform it into eternal *zoe*-life. Jesus makes it clear that His servants follow Him where He goes. We also must lay down our *psyche*-life so that others can experience *zoe*-life. It's in making this exchange, giving away our lives for others, that we discover ourselves to have *zoe*-life.[4]

Three Ways to Lay Down Your Life

> "Greater love has no one than this, than to *lay down* his life for his friends…" John 15:13

The Greek word *tithemi* is translated here as "lay down."

This is an appropriate translation, as Jesus is clearly speaking about His upcoming death. However, *tithemi* is the same word Jesus used in John 13 when He "put aside" his robe. It can mean to "lay down," "lay aside," or "lay up."

While literally dying for one another (laying down our lives) is

---

[3] Ephesians 2:8-10 "By grace you have been saved, through faith. And this is not your own doing; it is the gift of God, not as a result of works…for we are His workmanship, created…for good works."

[4] As is no doubt clear to the reader, this pattern of complete self-giving is based upon God's eternal inner life.

certainly a powerful expression of love, we can also lay down our lives for one another as we "lay aside" our lives on a day-to-day basis to benefit one another. We can also "lay up" our lives for one another in a similar way to how we store money, investing our lives for the benefit of one another.

In other words, obeying Jesus's New Commandment is not only limited to making the ultimate sacrifice for one another. We can, as Paul said, "die daily" in obedience to Jesus and out of love for one another by laying aside and laying up our lives for each other.

The Impact of Laying Aside Your Life

Jesus gets what He prays for. But it cost Him His life.

If we want to be part of the answer to Jesus's prayer, it will cost us our lives.

If it was good enough for the Master, it is good enough for us.

It is notable that of those who heard Jesus's words on that night, each and every one laid down their lives for one another, except the apostle John. Although the Romans tried multiple times to kill him, they were not able to, and he lived to a ripe old age. His hour had not yet come.

When someone lays aside their *psyche*-life (sacrifices for you), lays up their life (invests in you or for you), or lays down their life (gives their entire life for you), it communicates powerfully to us in a language beyond words.

"This person values me more than their own life. My life must be valuable." It creates a debt that can never be repaid, inspiring others to lay down their lives. If Jesus (the Master) died for my brother or sister, how much more so should I lay down my life for them? After all, Jesus's life was so much more valuable than mine.

A community that consistently lays aside, lays up, and lays down their lives for one another looks like the Trinity. The trinitarian life is revealed, once and for all, on the cross.

Dead Ends: Sacrifice without Love

In 1 Corinthians 13:3, Paul gives us an important warning about laying down our lives:

> "If I give away all I have, and if I deliver my body to be burned, but have not love, I gain nothing."

The person described here appears to have followed Jesus to the letter, giving away their *psyche*-life in the form of all their possessions, and then making the ultimate sacrifice, their very life. And yet, according to the apostle, because they did it without love, their sacrifice is completely worthless. This person laid down their life, not for others, but for themselves. Can you imagine their regret on the day of judgment as they realize their extreme act of sacrifice was completely meaningless to God? They gave everything they had for nothing.

God wants us to lay down our lives *for one another*, not out of religious zeal or selfish ambition. This fulfills the new Commandment, "Love one another as I have loved you." Love means acting for the benefit of others. Our sacrificial love for one another must be "patient and kind…not arrogant or rude…not irritable or resentful…"[5] When we lay down our lives for each other, there must be "faith [in God] working through love [for others]"[6] or it doesn't count. For this reason, it is so important that we first learn to be loved by God before rushing in to make our sacrifice. Truly, "we love because He first loved us."[7] Let us not be found like Cain, offering a sacrifice that does not please God.

---

5   1 Cor. 13:4-5
6   Galatians 5:6
7   1 John 4:19

Dead Ends: Victim not Volunteer

In John's Gospel, Jesus makes the repeated claim that no one is taking His life from Him. Instead, He is laying it down voluntarily.

> "For this reason, the Father loves me, because I lay down (*tithemi*) my *psyche*-life that I may take it up again. No one takes it from me, but I lay it down (*tithemi*) of my own accord. I have authority to lay it down and authority to take it up again."[8] John 10:17-18

Jesus is not a victim. No one is taking His life from Him. He is a volunteer, walking in obedience to His Father, and giving up His life as a free-will offering.

He is looking for other volunteers, those who will willingly lay down their lives.

There is no spiritual value in losing your life as a victim. Victims do not lay down their lives—they have them taken away from them, whether all at once or taken day-by-day. Of course, there is justice due to victims from God. But losing your life in this way does not participate in the form of Jesus's sacrifice.

In following Jesus, it is very common to begin as a volunteer and then wake up one day to realize a change has taken place. At some point, perhaps without knowing it, you stopped giving your life away freely. You have become a victim and others are taking your life without your permission. Just as sacrifice without love is meaningless, similarly, having your life stolen from you brings no eternal profit.

In following Jesus, we must also make sure that we are volunteers, giving our lives freely, rather than victims, being robbed of life by others. While the victim and the volunteer may look similar from the outside, they are radically different paths. Jesus calls us to be volunteers, not

---

8   See also Jesus before Pilate, John 19:11. Jesus also demonstrates His ability to escape those who arrested Him in the garden (John 18).

victims. As Psalm 110 prophesies of the Messiah, "Your people will volunteer freely on the day of your power…"

Dead Ends: A Sacrifice Out of Season

The cross is the ultimate collision of heaven and earth, the moment where the veil of God's inner life was torn open. However, most of Jesus's earthly life was not the cross. In the Gospel of John, Jesus repeatedly claims "my hour has not yet come." He knew there was a moment, a fullness of time, when His ultimate sacrifice was to take place.

Until then, He died daily, living a life of humility, service, and obedience to the Father.

Similarly, for us, there is a temptation in religious zeal to make large sacrifices for God that are not in obedience to God and not in His timing. Most days of our lives will look normal. We will eat, sleep, work, and serve. We must do all these things while learning to "lay aside" and "lay up" our lives for others.

Making a life-altering sacrifice on a day when all God wants us to do is water the garden is not spiritual, it is stupid.

However, at some moments in the fullness of time, there will be opportunities for greater sacrifices. Let's not be hasty and rush ahead to these moments. At the same time, we must be ready to meet them when they come. After all, "the one who loves me will follow me, and where I am, my servant will also be." Our lives of sacrificial love must stay in step with the seasons of God's grace.

Becoming Bread and Wine for One Another

At the end of the age, the great multitude of worshipers from Revelation 7 who walk in John 17 unity will emerge from the great tribulation. In Revelation 12:11, we see this same group of people from Revelation 7 achieve ultimate victory over the accuser. They triumph "by the blood of the Lamb and by the word of their testimony, *for they loved not their lives even unto death.*"

Their testimony is that, like the Lamb, they loved not their lives unto death. The have taken their *psyche*-life and transformed it into *zoe*-life. It's the blood of the Lamb combined with their own testimony, a testimony that has taken on the shape and form of His testimony, that overcomes Satan once and for all. The mature multitude of Revelation has learned from the Master. They've followed Him as their Shepherd and walked wherever He walked. As He became bread and wine for them, they have become bread and wine for one another.

This multitude in Revelation is the fullness of what Jesus prayed for in John 17. They are one as the Father and Son are one because they lay down their lives for one another, just as Father and Son fully give themselves to one another. If we want to see the fullness of what Jesus prayed for in John 17, we will have to meet Him at the cross. It's the place where Heaven and Earth meet, the place of glory, the place where we are brought into the inner life of God.

Just as His life is for us, so our lives must be for one another. This is the new commandment, "love one another as I have loved you," and it's the only way Jesus's prayer can be answered in fullness, "Let them be one, just as we are one."

Do you want to see an answer to His prayer? His life was the cost.

Now it's your turn.

He is inviting you, *"Lay down your life."*

Acknowledgments

I want to thank a number of people who contributed to this book.

To Matthew Lilley and the entire team at Presence Pioneers Media, thank you. It is such an honor to work and serve together on a weekly basis. Matthew, you always seem to have the right name. Honour Fraiser, thank you for the cover design and for all your help with pre-sales (aside from the innumerable other ways you help me). Jeffrey Pelton, your servant-heart, editing work, and introduction to the publishing world have been invaluable. I still can't remember where the quotation marks go, but I'm glad you know. Jenny Lester, thank you for your editing help. Our conversations and your suggestions were incredibly helpful in crafting the book. I could not have done it without you. Gaylord, thank you for the foreword and for your book *Love Revolution* which brought many of these concepts into greater focus years ago and for consistently modeling what it means to "Love one Another."

I'm grateful to many of my friends and partners through 10 Days, Global Family, and the New England Alliance who have shared this dream of John 17 unity and consistently model what it looks like to lay down your life. I am grateful for my children, Gabriel, Sabbath, Eva, Josie, Melchizedek, and Phineas. Most of all, I'm thankful to my wife, Cassi Friz, for being a constant help, support, and friend in ministry and all of life (Prov. 19:14).

JOIN THE MOVEMENT

FIND OUT MORE AT
10DAYS.NET

Have questions?
10DaysCommunications@gmail.com

Visit Our Website
www.10Days.net

Check out these other titles by Presence Pioneers Media

   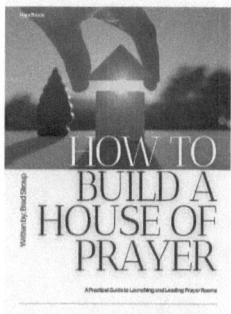

10 DAYS
by Jonathan Friz

ENJOYING PRAYER
by Matthew Lilley

DAVID'S TABERNACLE
by Matthew Lilley

HOW TO BUILD A HOUSE OF PRAYER
by Brad Stroup

Available wherever you buy books or at
presencepioneers.org

To get updates and discounts on future book releases visit media.presencepioneers.org or scan the QR code below